First Hardcover Edition, November 2020.

Library of Congress Control Number: 2020921212

ISBN#: 978-1-7353986-2-4

"Remember the days of old,

consider the years of many generations:

ask thy parents, and they will show thee;

thy elders, and they will tell thee."

Deuteronomy 32:7

Introduction

Mabel Isabel Dove (1880-1957), an early feminist leader and founder of the Morgantown, West Virginia chapter of the NAACP, was a devoted Christian who, along with her husband, ministered to the people of West Virginia for over thirty years.

This anthology contains her biography, details regarding her ancestry, and a collection of some of her essays and poems that she wrote throughout the seasons of her fruitful life. I hope this book will bring her works to life and that her literary talents and ministry will be remembered forever.

Yehuda "J.R." Rothstein
New York, New York
November 1, 2020

TABLE OF CONTENTS

PART I

THE LIFE & ANCESTRY OF MABEL ISABEL DOVE

By J.R. Rothstein
Based upon the research of Catherine Dove Gibbs-Robertson

Mabel Isabel Dove (1880-1957) was born on June 13, 1880, in Grand Rapids, Michigan. She is the third of five children born to Dr. Solon Willet Dove (1850-1934) and Julia Adelia McClure (1854-1927). Mabel's maternal grandparents were Orrin McClure (1818-1894) and Elizabeth Patterson (1826-1868). Mabel's paternal grandparents were Daniel Griffen Dove (1828-1910) and Ruth Elizabeth Beers[1] (1832-1911).

The Story of Daniel Griffen Dove - Civil War Hero

Mabel's paternal grandfather, Daniel Griffen Dove, no doubt played a role in Mabel's imagination.

Daniel Griffen Dove (1828-1910) is a man whose origins and story have been one of intrigue and mystery for generations of Dove historians and genealogists[2]. Nothing is known about him or his family

---

[1] Ruth is a descendant of Daniel Beers (1726-1801), who fought with 2ndMassachusetts Regulars in the American Revolution under John Bailey; Cornelius Dykeman (1707-1783), who was accused of being hostile to the cause of independence during the American Revolution evolution because he criticized the new Continental currency; Daniel Tourner, an original Dutch settler of Harlem, New York; numerous founding settlers of both Hartford, and Norwalk, Connecticut, including Ralph Keeler (1613 -1672), an ancestor of many prominent individuals in American history, including United States Presidents.

[2] Many theories have been put forth over the generations about Daniel G. Dove and theories regarding his origins have been ripe with speculation. Catherine Gibbs believed that Daniel had African-American ancestry although DNA results show that theory without any basis. The

except that Daniel's father may have been named Louis and he may have been from Scotland. Daniel Griffen is said to have been born on May 7, 1828, in either Greenwich, Connecticut or New York. He married Ruth Elizabeth Beers on April 22, 1828, in Ridgefield, Connecticut when he was 21. Ruth (1832-1911) was a girl from an established and early New England family whose genealogy is well-known in the annals of New England history. Daniel "followed farming as his occupation until the war of 1861, when he answered the call for volunteers."

At the age of 34, during the height of the American Civil War, Daniel volunteered to fight to preserve the union from the treachery. He joined the 17th Connecticut Volunteer Infantry as a Private in a regiment that served in the Union Army during the American Civil War. He registered for the infantry at the nearby town of Bridgeport on August 13, 1862, and was assigned to Company G. He marched out toward the front lines on August 28, 1862, under the command of Colonel William H. Noble. Daniel was almost five feet six and had fair skin, brown eyes, and brown hair. A man named William Dove, possibly a relative, mustered out with him. Among the many men of the 17th were relatives of his wife, Ruth.

Daniel left behind five children in Connecticut to be raised alone by Ruth, who, in his absence, must have catered to their children's education. In addition to leaving behind a young wife, Daniel left at home two-year-old Anna Bell (1860-), three-year-old Ida (1857-), six-year-old John Willet[3] (1854-1934), Mabel's father, eight-year-old Cyrus

---

author posits, without any substance, that Daniel Griffen Dove was not his birth name. A griffin is a mystical flying creature and perhaps the name was adopted later or that the whole name Griffen Dove, in general, was adopted by a young man that appears out of nowhere in the historical record in 1850, to marry Ruth Beers.

[3] There is some discrepancy as to whether John Willet was born in 1850 or 1854. Daniel Dove's Civil War application lists Solon W.'s birthday as December 9, 1854, which would make Solon the middle child. However, other records place the date as 1850 which would make Solon W. the eldest child.

Griffen (1852-1916), and nine-year-old Irving Berlin (1851-1911). Daniel and Ruth had lost twin boys[4] at birth a few years earlier and, no doubt, Ruth's separation from her husband must have been particularly difficult for her. Whatever the character of the man in August of 1862, his experience in the American Civil War would change him forever.

According to the Adjutant General's Office of the War Department's military report dated October 28, 1886, Daniel would have an eventful yet traumatic military service. On May 2, 1863, at the Battle of Chancellorsville, Virginia, Daniel was captured and sent to Libby Prison in Richmond, Virginia. Libby Prison was a Confederate prison during the American Civil War. The prison gained an infamous reputation for its overcrowded and harsh conditions under which the officer prisoners from the Union Army were kept. Daniel would have been exposed to prisoners who suffered from diseases, malnutrition, and with a high mortality rate. By mid-1863, when Daniel arrived at the prison, one thousand prisoners crowded into large open rooms on two floors with open, barred windows, leaving them exposed to weather and temperature extremes.

From Libby Prison, Daniel was sent to numerous parole camps. The parole camps, for the most part, were a result of the parole system where captured soldiers pledged not to fight. In the days of formal warfare, it was customary to exchange prisoners of war by a complex formula of numbers and relative rank. To avoid being burdened with large parties of prisoners, forces in the field would often "parole" them, that is to release them to go home on oath, not to perform any military service until they were exchanged. Early in the Civil War, it was discovered that many paroled men would disappear into the civilian population, not to be found when ready for exchange. So, keeping them under military control until they were exchanged and returned to their

---

[4] Perhaps only one died either during or within two weeks of childbirth.

6

units became imperative. It was in one of these parole camps that Daniel G. Dove found himself presumably waiting to be restored to a combat role if some prisoners of war were traded to the other side.

A military report follows of the Adjutant General's Office of the War Department dated October 28, 1886, concerning Daniel:

Respectfully returned to the Commissioner of Pensions Daniel G. Dove, a Private of Company G, 17th Regiment Connecticut Infantry Volunteers, was enrolled on the 13th day of August, 1862, at Ridgefield for 3 years and is reported on the muster rolls of Connecticut from August 28, 1862, (date of muster in) to April 30, 1863, present; May and June 1863, absent paroled prisoner; same is August 31, 1863; September & October 1863, present; same is February 29, 1863; March & April 1864, absent; no remark. Regiment reports for March 1864, reports him absent in [intelligible]. . . on daily duty [intelligible]. Roll for May and June 1864, present; same to June 30, 1865. Mustered out a Corporal with Co. at Hilton-Head, SC July 19, 1865.

Regiment report for May 1863, reports him missing in action, May 2, 1863, supposed to be paroled; Regiment was in action at Chancellorsville, Va. May 2, 1863; Ret. For January, 1864, does not report him absent. He was captured at Chancellorsville, Va. May 3, 1863, confined at Richmond, Va. May 9, 1863, paroled at City-Paint, Va. May 14, 1863, reported at College Green Barracks, Maryland, May 16, 1863, reported at Camp Parole, Maryland same day, sent to Washington, D.C. May 20, 1863, was received at Parole Camps, Va. May 21, 1863, and present at Camp Convalescent, Va. May 29, 1863, on the records he appears as deserted since May 25, 1863. This charge of desertion is removed as erroneous. He appears to have been sent from Camp Convalescent, Va. date not stated, to Parole Camp,

Va. from which camp he was sent to Camp Distribution, Va. October 4, 1863, and from the latter camp to his regiment, which he rejoined October 21, 1863.

Company morning reports show him June 4, 1863, from missing in action, October 21, 1863, returned from Parole Camp to the regiment. Company release for July 1863, shows him as absent, wounded, and paroled; so, borne on return for August & September 1863. Regimental hospital records show him admitted November 4, 1863, with diarrhea and excused Dec. 30, 1863. The records of this office furnish no evidence of alleged disabilities.

Gettysburg photographer William Tipton shot this image of the dedication of the 17th Connecticut monument on July 1, 1884.

In July 1863, the 17th Connecticut began its campaign at Gettysburg, Pennsylvania, in what would be the defining battle not only of the unit but for the Civil War. Others who were captured simultaneously with Daniel at Chancellorsville were released in time to rejoin the unit at Gettysburg. It isn't clear from the record whether Daniel fought at Gettysburg, or was alternatively sitting in a Confederate prison, and the issue needs further research. Whether at Gettysburg or in a prison, the experience must have been exceptionally difficult for him and he must have been a witness to many horrible sites. The confusion of the record regarding whether Daniel had deserted his unit during the summer of 1863, has caused Daniel much anxiety. It must have taken some effort to set the record straight. Daniel's station and the overall condition appears to have improved as the war went on. He got honorably discharged at the rank of Corporal in July 1865.

Pensions records provide that after that war, Daniel returned home to Connecticut, presumably to Ridgefield. Daniel then spent "one year at Danbury in 1870, [then] moved to Grand Rapids, Michigan and from there to Nowego, Michigan, then to Cedar Springs, Michigan." Daniel's obituary provides some insight into the last years of his life:

> *In 1870, with his family, [Daniel and Ruth] came to Michigan, choosing Cedar Springs as their home, where he has resided since. [Daniel] followed draying [a dray is a low cart without fixed sides, used for carrying heavy loads] as a business for many years. Until later in life, he retired from active business. Mr. Dove was converted under the preaching of Rev. J. Malcomb Smith of the Congregational Society and was a member as long as the society remained. He was a much-respected citizen, quiet and loving in all his dealing with his fellow man. A high standard of character to leave to his bereaved family and friends. . . Rev. Carrick gave a very appropriate discourse to a large number of sympathizing friends. Interment in the family lot in Elmwood Cemetery. The family feels very grateful to neighbors and friends for the many acts of*

kindness shown to them in their sad bereavement, and also to the Masons for many favors.

Dr. Solon W. Dove & Julia Adelia McClure

It is also from the story of Mabel's grandfather, Daniel, that we can deduce a bit about John Willet Dove, Mabel's father. John Willet, and his brother, Cyrus Arthur Dove, became wealthy, educated physicians. Dr. John W. Dove was said to have also conducted business and was socially and politically conservative. At some point in life, John Willet changed his name to Solon W., perhaps after the famous doctor of antiquity[5]. On October 30, 1872, at the age of 17, John Willet married Julia Adelia McClure, also 17, in Grand Rapids, Michigan. Julia was the daughter of Orrin McClure (1818-1894) and Elizabeth Patterson (1821-1868).

Julia Adelia had come from a tumultuous past and had many difficulties in her life, which she overcame. Julia's mother, Elizabeth, had died in 1868, when she was only 13 years old. Her father, Orin, at age 19, drove cattle from Rutland, Vermont to Buffalo, New York and then later emigrated to Michigan where he was called a "blue bellied Yankee." Orin later suffered a terrible accident, having fallen off a horse and buggy, and was never the same again. Orin ultimately died of "insanity" in 1894. Julia's brother, George, had fought in the civil war for the union.

---

[5] No biographical research has been obtained on Dr. Solon Dove. The obituary of his brother, however, Cyrus Dove provides that "Cyrus J. Dove, who is a native of Connecticut, born on December 15, 1853, in Stamford, Fairfield County. His parents, Daniel and Ruth (Beers) Dove, were natives also of the Nutmeg State, and the father was a man of means."

The family of Orin and Elizabeth had been split up when Elizabeth died. Julia's sister, Charlotte, was sent to live with an aunt, Sarah McClure Rose, and her husband, Willard, before being sent to live with another relative, Arthur McClure and his wife, Mattie, of Rutland, Vermont. The author is under the impression that it was Elizabeth who sang to her children, including Julia, the bedtime song, *Run Along Home* which has been transmitted in the Dove family for nearly two centuries.

The rhyme, which Julia Adelia sang to her daughter Mabel, goes as follows: "Run along home, and jump into bed, close your eyes, and cover your head, the very same thing, I say unto you, you dream of me, and I'll dream of you." The song, in general, seems to have played a large role in Julia Adelia's upbringing and she and her siblings would sing together as they engaged in chores. Julia did the same thing when she raised her own children.

Arthur McClure and his wife Mattie, outside their home in Rutland, Vermont.
Date unknown.

Charlotte McClure Walker.
Date and location unknown.

Julia Adelia McClure.
Date and location unknown.

Mabel's Early Years

Solon W. and Julia had five children in Kent Township, Grand Rapids, Michigan: (1) Arthur Cyrus Dove (1874-1933); (2) Mattie Elizabeth Dove (1877-1884); (3) Mabel Isabel Dove (1880-1957); (4) Solon W. Dove Jr. (1882-1883); and (5) Ruth Dove (1884-1884).

A poem written by Mabel Dove on Mother's Day May 13, 1951, gives some insight into the ethos of the home that Julia Adelia created with Dr. Dove. The poem, entitled Memories of Mother, is as follows:

Memories of Mother

I'm thinking at the twilight hour,
Of her, my mother dear,
Of how we met for family prayer,
God's sacred word to hear.

'Twas there I learned of God's great power,
His wondrous love and care,
That follow me where e'er I go —
For God is everywhere.

She taught us too, the Jesus Way
Of getting on with others,
And how He wants us to be True,
To treat them all as brothers.

I think how cheerfully she served
And cared for us each day —
For all she was, and meant to me,
Love's tribute I would pay!
     — Mabel D. Gibbs

Mother's Day
5-13-51

14

I'm thinking at the twilight hour
Of her, my mother dear
Of how we met for family prayer,
God's sacred word to hear.

'Twas there I learned of God's Great power,
His wondrous love and care,
That follow me where e'er I go–
For God is everywhere.

She taught us too, the Jesus way
Of getting on with other,
And how he wants us to be true,
To treat them all as brothers.

I think how cheerfully she served
And cared for us each day –
For all she was, and meant to me,
Love's tribute I would pay!

It would be Julia Adelia's faith that would help guide her family through difficult times. It is also ironic that despite Dr. Dove being a physician and homoeopathist[6], he and his family experienced a great many illnesses, well beyond Dr. Dove's ability to control, and which resulted in the deaths of three of five of his children. The Dove family bible contains some insight into the plagues which brought devastation unto the Dove house. The bible entries, likely inscribed by Dr. Dove himself but possibly by Julia Adelia McClure, provide the following account:

> *Arthur C. Dove had whooping cough in February of 1879, had dys[entria] diarrhea in July of 1880; was vaccinated in July of 1880. I had Koine Pox. Mattie G. had whooping cough in Feb. of 1879. I had Calark (sp) fever very severe in December 1878; was vaccinated successfully in January of 1882. Arthur had measles moderately in the Spring of 1883. Mattie had measles very hard in the Spring of 1883. Mabel had measles in the Spring of 1883, and all had the meningitis the same Spring before, they had the measles. Solon Jr. had boils all Spring and Summer until about the 12th of July when he had cholera, influenza, and was sick about 1 week and died on the 17th.*

According to Dove family historian, Catherine Gibbs, "Mattie, Mabel, and Solon had severe cerebral spinal meningitis. Only Mabel survived. Her hands and spine are weak for the rest of her life, which she refused to accept. Mabel employed all known scientific methods to strengthen herself [and engaged in] swimming, [proto] yoga, healthy food, [a managed] diet, [and was influenced by the teachings of] Dr. Frank McCoy."

---

[6] No record has been found to date to confirm that Dr. Solon W. attended medical school. A record, however, for his brother does exist.

The surviving members of the Dove Family. Top: Arthur Dove and Mabel Dove. Bottom: Solon W. Dove and Julia Adelia McClure. Chattanooga, Tennessee. Circa 1898.

Arthur Cyrus Dove, The Rebel

Mabel was a studious and gifted student. From a young age, she was called to public service and public life. One of her earliest causes was the fight against alcohol consumption. The zeal in which Mabel displayed for the cause throughout her life has led the author, David Shepherd, and Catherine Gibbs to speculate with a reasonable basis that the abuse of alcohol was present in Mabel's family of origins. The author believes that the origins lay in her experience with her brother.

It was believed that alcohol has been consumed and abused by Mabel's rebellious older brother, Arthur Cyrus McClure. Arthur was described as an unfocused wanderer. According to Catherine Gibbs, "Arthur Cyrus changed his name to Arthur McClure Dove." He had married a woman, which research has revealed as Florence Reeves, and then shortly thereafter divorced her. Arthur then married again to a second woman named Marie. The Dove family, including Mabel, was so upset by the divorce, and particularly by the choice of the second wife, that Mabel [and likely her parents] broke off communication with Arthur. Arthur's lifestyle also seemed to be a contributing factor in this decision.

The second wife of Arthur was apparently a "scandalous" woman because she wore make-up and drank alcohol, both of which Mabel and her family found objectionable. Marie may also be associated with the arts and may have had an unstable personality, but this cannot be confirmed. According to Catherine Gibbs, "mother never forgave the divorce (which was totally unacceptable in that day) and cut him out of her life. His wife [Marie] wrote of his death [and that there had been a child. The letter was discovered when Mabel's daughter, Marjorie, had gone into her father's study snooping and discovered the letter and its contents which described the child.] Mabel was heartbroken [regarding Arthur's death] and took to her room for a whole day and night. How all four of us [Gibbs children] wish we could find this child's name – our cousin. . . . Arthur died November 4, 1933, in Naukin Township, Wayne County, Michigan, home address 9421 North Lawn, Detroit,

Michigan of a cerebral hemorrhage." Catherine Gibbs, Kim Depwitt, David Shepherd, Curtis Robertson, and the author, have spent significant time researching the life of Arthur, his wives, and have discovered no record of a child. Catherine Gibbs submitted DNA results to numerous databases prior to her death, in the hopes that Arthur's child would want to learn of his roots and would also submit a DNA sample to the same database. However, as of this date, no child has been located.

Arthur McClure Dove. Date and location unknown.

Mabel Participates in the Experiment of Female Higher Education

By the age of 17, Mabel had blossomed into a studious, principled, public service-oriented teenager. Mabel developed hostility to the consumption of alcohol and became a supporter of the temperance movement. Mabel, believing in fairness for women, supported the suffrage movement and its goal for greater civil rights for the fair sex. Mabel was active in her church and took her biblical faith seriously. Mabel finished high school by age 16 and had done much to cultivate her mind throughout her childhood.

Mabel wanted to attend university but the options for higher education for women during the era were limited. Mabel ultimately settled on Chattanooga Normal University for women and was one of the forty-three students of the 1897 commencing class of the University. By 1896, the entire Dove family relocated from Michigan to Chattanooga, Tennessee, possibly to accommodate Mabel and her desire to pursue higher education. It is likely that from the perspective of Dr. Dove and Julia, Mabel was the most promising of the two remaining children.

The following photos were taken during her time at university:

Mabel Isabel Dove. 1897.

Will Armstrong
Boston.

Augusta Converse, a close friend of Mabel Dove.
Chattanooga, Tennessee. Circa 1898.

Mabel and classmates at a home of Augusta Converse.
Monday, November 13, 1899. Chattanooga, Tennessee.

Mabel Dove and friend. Normal University, South Bank of
Campus. Chattanooga, Tennessee. 1898

Mabel and friends playing pranks on one another. Normal
University, Chattanooga, Tennessee. Circa 1898.

Umbrella Rock. Lookout Point. March 28, 1898.
Chattanooga, Tennessee.

Mabel graduated from university within three years and was designated as the class valedictorian. Mabel's speech, given at her commencement on May 24, 1900, was published in local newspapers and was very well received at the time. It has been studied by generations of her descendants.

What Mabel did after graduation is unknown, but there is a possibility that she taught in local schools. After graduation, Mabel lived with her family in a large, expensive home near the university. Mabel and her father, who had become a well-known physician, socialized among the social elite of the city.

Mabel Dove with family and friends. July 4, 1903, Chattanooga, Tennessee.

Mabel Meets The Love Of Her Life

It was during this period that Mabel met Bernard Gibbs, a divinity student at the University of Chattanooga, who had a part-time job as a milkman to pay for expenses.

One day, while on his route delivering milk, which Bernard did on a horse and carriage, he met Mabel Isabel Dove. Bernard courted Mabel in the traditional Victorian manner. Bound by Victorian and conservative Christian norms, Bernard sent Mabel love letters and took advantage of the milk route to encounter Mabel. The couple fell very much in love with one another. Bernard was likely taken by the strong-willed, principled, and talented valedictorian of Normal University, who shared her deep passion and love of the gospel. Mabel was likely taken by the handsome orator who spoke of justice and of creating a utopian world.

A surviving poem by Mabel gives some insight into their courtship:

A Cherished Reminiscence, a memory fond – you say?
Well here is one: – A man, a mid, a dreamy summer's day.
A ride beyond the city's heart, with kindly chaperone,
A winding mountain road, a jest, a match of merry tune.
A halt beside a sparkling stream, a hunt for flowrets care,
A knightly man, a laughing maid, a wild rose in her hair.
A dainty lunch, then chaperone doth dose, doth take a nap,
The while, with book of poesy, the man and maid chat.
A story told, the birds o'erheard ecstatic music make
As they behold, eyes meet, hands clasp, lips-sh!
Chaperone's awake!

Bernard Gibbs and Mabel Dove.
December 5, 1904. Chattanooga, Tennessee.

Despite their great affection for one another, oral history suggests that Mabel's family was initially not as enthusiastic about the match as she. The family preferred that Mabel select someone from their class and sphere of society. Nevertheless, the couple overcame whatever obstacles were presented and, according to Catherine Gibbs, got married on Bernard's birthday, December 5, 1904. Mabel's family and friends teased Mabel for the rest of her life for 'marrying down' and for falling in love with the milkman. Upon their marriage, Mabel, seeing how important the cause of Methodism was to Bernard, agreed to join his Church despite her deep ties to the Congregationalist Church, which one of her ancestors had helped found.

Mabel, being the daughter of Dr. Dove, brought political and economic resources to Bernard's ministry. Dr. Dove liquidated his holdings in Michigan and Tennessee and then purchased some land out in Oakland, California, and also provided a home for Mabel and her Bernard. Dr. Dove also helped Bernard get his first job. On the weekends, the couple would travel north to Dr. Dove's estate where, as a gentleman rancher, he had horses and fruit trees.

Mabel Raises Her Children & Takes On The Role Of A Minister's Wife

At the beginning of her marriage, Mabel followed her husband from location to location but frequently returned to Anaheim, California to tend to her parents with her two young children. At the homestead or in any other location in which Mabel found herself, she developed a highly structured and disciplined regime. Mabel managed her children, her husband, and at the same time, kept up the appearances and obligations of a minister's wife. Despite the tremendous pressure that Mabel felt, she was very affectionate towards her children, often writing them love letters and poems in their honor.

Mabel Dove and Bernard Gibbs with baby Marjorie Dove Gibbs.
1910, Boyle Heights, Los Angeles, California.

Left to right: unknown, Julia Adelia McClure, Dr. Solon W. Dove, Mabel
Dove. Children are Julie Gibbs and Marge Gibbs. Anaheim, California.
Circa 1916.

Mabel Dove Gibbs, Marge Gibbs, and
Julie. Anaheim, California, 1916-1917.

This structure helped Mabel in the arduous circumstance of being separated from her husband for extended periods of time as he preached. In one letter written to Bernard on February 24, 1927, Mabel captures this separation as follows:

Got your splendid letters of 18ᵗʰ some days before.

Dear Heart,

The way is surely hard, but faint not. I feel as you do – you must not come unless your place is secure. Better separation for a time than bitterness, discouragement, and starvation. I could not stand it if I not rushed along, too busy to think by day, too tired at night to stay awake and brood. John said, "Won't it be just wonderful when we have our daddy back? How deeply we all echoed that!

As a mother, this disciplined nature would direct Mabel to develop a daily routine for both for herself and children, which included whole grains and exercise. Mabel would wake her children daily shortly after dawn. She would usher them out of the home outside where she would make them do calisthenics, even if it was cold outside. Because Mabel was militant in her pursuit of healthy eating and fitness, being heavily influenced by the Kellog movement of natural eating, she zealously pursued these practices to her children's bewilderment. Elsewhere, before bed each night and after she had a shampoo, Mabel would comb her long hair exactly a hundred strokes. She would then clean the brush out and save the hair to make pillows.

Mabel was an avid writer of poetry and a master of verse. She would use this skill set to assist her husband in his ministerial capacities by writing poetry and letters to congregants that may have lost a loved one, or by assisting her husband in his sermons. After Mabel's mother, Julia Adelia, died in 1927, her father, Dr. Dove, remarried a woman named Helen. A poem written by Mabel in honor of her mother gives the reader a sense of her style.

Mabel's poem entitled "In Mother's Garden" is as follows:

I walked in my Mother's garden,
Sore bereft, at the close of the day.
And my heart was heavy and pained with grief–
God had summoned the gardener away!

But the flowers still bloomed in the beauty,
Bright visions of color and form.
So fragile, their petals might fall at a touch,
Or fade at the breath of a storm.

My heart questioned why, in its sorrow,
Must this being of brightness and worth
Thus vanish in pain from our presence away,
Yet frail flowers adorn still the earth.

Came the answer: "As on earth, so in Heaven,
There is need for hearts, loving and true,
As she and her flowers spread comfort and cheer
She, in Heaven, gives sweet service too.

"My heart then felt solace and comfort
As I thought she was now free from pain,
And yet serving the Master with gladness and love,
Please God, I would follow her train!

When Mabel's father, Dr. Dove, died, no will had been found among his papers. Oral and written history indicate that Mabel was disappointed and suspicious towards Dr. Dove's second wife, Helen, regarding the circumstances of the disposition of Dr. Dove's estate and wealth—specifically the large silver mines which Dr. Dove owned in California. Some of these papers can be reviewed in the Dove family archive.

Bernard And Mabel Maintained Their Love Throughout Their Marriage & Raised Close Children

The Gibbs children spoke about the great love and respect that existed between Bernard and Mabel, two traits that defined their marriage. Bernard and Mabel would buy one another gifts and often engage in romantic gestures. Sometimes, they would play pranks on one another. In one instance, Catherine Gibbs recalls that Bernard placed a brown paper bag on the kitchen table, which he first had blown up. Knowing that Bernard often placed gifts for her in such bags, Mabel approached the bag and assumed it was another gift for her. But when she opened it, the bag was empty. She cried out "Bernard!" in a tone of "how could you?" but it was all very playful. In Victorian society, it was not acceptable for spouses to show affection in front of children. But Catherine recalls seeing them once embracing in the hallway, so loving and tender and gentle with one another.

It was no doubt Mabel's deep love for Bernard that permitted her, throughout Bernard's life and throughout their mission, to stand by her husband's side. Mabel, despite not sharing all of Bernard's unusual views, supported his ministry while loving, honoring, and respecting her husband. Mabel followed Bernard through difficult times. The couple suffered financially from loss of prestige, and Bernard received threats against him and his family because of his activism. Throughout it all, despite her privileged background, Mabel was never afraid to roll up her sleeves and do what needed to be done for God and the church. Their shared commitment to a life of public service was a cornerstone of their marriage. Their similar temperaments meant that they fit very well together. This preserved their romance into old age, and as Mabel's writings indicate, even beyond Bernard's death.

Mabel and Bernard had a strong sense of humor which was

The Gibbs Family. From left to right: Catherine, Bernard, Mabel, Margery, John, and Julia. Morgantown, West Virginia, 1944.

something adopted by their children. Mabel's two younger children, John and Catherine, were born when Mabel was 42 and 44 respectively, providing a large age gap between her two other children. Once, John and Catherine overheard two parishioners observing the large age gap between the two older siblings and the two younger children. The younger children responded, perhaps intending to create a scandal, that "the older siblings are from Rev. Gibbs's first marriage." The two would attempt to tell the truth with the intent to deceive. Due to the large age gap, Marge helped deliver Catherine and also helped raise her younger siblings.

Mabel also took an active interest in her children's dating life and tried to break up relationships which she felt were bad for them. For example, Mabel broke up a relationship that Catherine had with a local West Virginia boy before she moved to Chicago to attend Northwestern. Mabel also broke up a relationship that her daughter Julia had with a Jewish man—who Julia claimed was the love of her life—and for which Julia never forgave her mother.

The Last Years

In 1942, after Bernard retired from the ministry, the couple was forced to live in a small apartment stationed above Tony Carony's grocery store in Morgantown, West Virginia. During this period, because Reverend Gibbs had no stipend from the church, Mabel worked as a house mother at a sorority at the university across the Wesley Methodist Church to stay out of poverty. Bernard went to work as a shoe salesman at Morrison Shoe Store.

Marge married Jim Shepherd and shortly after, Jim went overseas to serve in World War II. Marge moved into Bernard and Mabel's home with her young son, David Wendell Shepherd. David was partially raised by Mabel and often felt as if he was the fifth Gibbs child.

After the war, Marge, Mabel, and Jim pulled their savings, including some money left after Bernard's death, and put a down payment on the house at 225 Euclid Ave in Morgantown West, Virginia. David recalls going with his mother, Marjorie Gibbs Shepherd, and grandmother Mabel to look at the house. He recalls Marge and Mabel cleaning the home, moving the dining room table into the property, and preparing to make it a home.

David also recalls that as Mabel aged, her health deteriorated and she had many strokes. Over time, she became more and more confined to her bedroom on the second floor. It was hard for Mabel to move and she couldn't go up or down the stairs easily. Marge honored her mother and would take food up to her and took good care of Mabel. Despite this, Mabel and Marge had enough energy and zeal to defend baby David against the social ills of society. These women would review magazines together and pull out all of the alcohol and cigars advertisements, and destroy them. This was to ensure that young David would not be exposed to any ill influences and the evils of addiction to which other family members had succumbed. Mabel was a very religious woman and her daughter Marjorie once remarked that Mabel "would do anything that would help get her into heaven." And towards that end, Mabel spent the last years of her life doing everything in her power to ensure that she, and her children, would be in heaven together.

Mabel Isabel Dove died on March 9, 1957, in Morgantown, West Virginia, when she was 76 years old. She was buried next to her husband in East Oak Grove Cemetery in Morgantown, Monongalia County, West Virginia.

PART II

THE VALEDICTORY SPEECH
OF MABEL ISABEL DOVE

The Valedictory Speech of Mabel Dove
Normal University, May 24, 1900

Miss Mabel Dove was the valedictorian of the evening. She is a girl of striking intellectuality, and the delivery of her address was harmonious with its fine conception. Her voice was pure, vibrant, and penetrating, being heard with the greatest ease. Her subject was an odd one: "The Gods Sell Us Everything For Toil," and she spoke as follows:

The Gods Sell Us Everything For Toil

The subject of the rewards of toil and perseverance is, by no means, a new one. Many of us have heard it discussed from earliest childhood, but with one the less force, it remains a vital practical truth, and will as long as man has the aspirations and will to attain them.

Tis the continued, steady effort that wins where superior advantages without determination and perseverance ignominiously fail. For "a falling drop at last will cave a stone." It is not the mere drop that wears the stone away, for the insignificant globule by a single fall would wear off a particle almost too infinitesimally small to conceive: but it is the constant falling that finally caves the stone.

Since the command went forth, as the primal pair left the gates of Eden, that man should eat his bread by the sweat of his brow, toil has been the price which the children of earth have paid for, aught desirable that they have obtained. Each has been subject to the same law, and as there has been no royal path to knowledge, likewise only labor's high way has led to eminence and success in all vocations of life. Perseverance, indefatigable energy, and labor have been the cause of which honor and success were the effects. Someone has said that "successful men owe more to their perseverance than to their natural powers, their friends, or to the favorable circumstance around them."

Thus, the masterly achievements of Julius Caesar were not the inevitable consequences of fated genius; they were the fruits of arduous and incessant exertion coupled, to be sure, with talent and ambition. Such a combination was an *open sesame* to fortune's door. "Genius unexerted, is no more genius then a bushel of acorns is a forest of oaks." So, if the genius of Michelangelo had not been united with strenuous effort, the world would have been less rich. For the immortal masterpieces of sculpture, which now ennoble the world of art, would have remained rough and senseless blocks of marble. The shining jewels buried deep in the earth's dark bosom, are brought to light only by the repeated blows of the miner's faithful pick. So, the priceless gems of truth may lie in the perpetual darkness, concealed from our view, unless we, by dint of toil and sedulous effort, exhume the crude stone and polish it into a radiant gem that shall be meant to shine upon the brow of posterity.

The eminent Dr. Arnold of Rugby, from his long experiences in training boys, said that "the difference between one boy and another was not so much in talent as in energy and determination." And truly, history abounds with examples of men who have reached their goal only because they willed it and worked for it. It is said when Disraeli, the great English Prime Minister, delivered his first speech in parliament. He made a dismal failure and was mercilessly laughed at and derided. Stung by the ridicule, he exclaimed, "You laugh at me now, but the time will come when you will hear me." And by patient industry, he verified his prediction. He forthwith set resolutely to work correcting his faults, studied assiduously, and practiced untiringly till he had mastered the art of oratory. Then those who had once laughed at him now acknowledged his power and sat spellbound under his eloquence. Thus, have man by tireless application accomplished marvels.

The numberless modern improvements and inventions which furnish us, comfort and convenience we thoughtlessly enjoy, forgetful of the cost at which they were procured, at a cost of years of diligent study, painstaking effort, and toil. Likewise, the advancement in learning and science is the result of careful research, concentrated thought, and persistent application. But success has not been attained in a day, nor yet in a year, but only by many days and many years of faithful and repeated action. But each year is composed of fleeting moments. Verily, life is made up of littles – of seeming trifles that insensibly form the warp and woof of our characters.

How we treat these small things, the flying moments, the little opportunities – how we live each day – will determine their influence on our lives, for "our days and yesterdays are the blocks with which we build." He who appreciates the value of time, and fills his odd moments with study, or with the pursuit of some high purpose will, at length, find himself rich in the possession of a well-stored and cultured mind, or happy in the accomplishment of some darling project. After the distinguished statesman Edmund Burke had finished one of his first eloquent speeches in the English parliament, his brother, speaking at the end of a thoughtful reverie, said, "I have been wondering how Ned has contrived to monopolize all the talent of the family: but then I remember when we're at play, he was always at work."

The sad mistake of idly dreaming of fame and longing for greatness is made by a man who might achieve it if they only set about it with the invincible determination to win. Without that, it will not come for, "Tis not in mortals to command success: let us do more – deserve it!" Again, many who wish for success are unwilling to battle against adverse circumstances and thinking effort useless, ignobly succumb to unfavorable conditions. Some of the most illustrious characters of history have been those who have risen and achieved great things against difficulties seemingly almost insuperable. Opposition has not baffled them – nay it seemed rather to strengthen their power of resistance. Though it is indeed true that the individual is influenced by circumstances, he need not be enthralled by them. I like the verse in which this thought is thus expressed:

> "Why become a slave of chance
> Why be crushed by circumstance?
> Rise above it and advance
> Overall adversity.
> You're a king and can create
> For yourself your own estate,
> You are master of your fate, you are free."

Free. Yes, free! Free, with all the grand future before us. It is ours – ours to make or to mar. Ah! If men whose powers have been only the mediocre talents that we possess, have risen to greatness, have bettered the world, and left to posterity a goodly heritage – are these, I say have risen, why, or why cannot we, the children of the fairer morn, the heirs of grander possibilities, make the world a little better or a little brighter for our having lived! It lies with us! Cassius voiced it truly when he said, "Men at some time are master of their fate; the fault, dear Brutus, is not in our stars, but in ourselves, that we are underlings."

Tis little at best we can do. Newton, after spending years in patient toil and giving to the world of science inestimable acquisitions, felt that what he had achieved was like a few shells gathered from the beach while the great ocean of truth lay unexplored before him. But we may not all be great. History may not blazon our names and deeds to be read of future generations. But at least, we can all labor to live, to have rich, abundant lives, to be – not underlings, but to rise to the full stature of god-like race, striving unceasingly for that which is best, rising "by stepping-stones of our dead selves, to high things."

But still, the moments come and go in their flight, they bring us many things, sorrow as well as joy, partings as well as glad meetings. The moment just now approaching brings a parting of the ways, and as valedictorian for the class of 1900 – long live the Century Class. I must now linger to say a few words of farewell. It seems sad that now in our

43

last glad moment of triumphant happiness we must pause to dash away a tear – tears of sorrow that we who have for many terms, together have trodden the thorny path toward knowledge, must now separate, most of us to go diverging ways, some to other schools of learning, others to the broader schools of practical experience. But as we go, it will be with pleasant memories of the years spent within these college halls, and with that preparation that shall help us to make our way through the world.

During our time of preparing, I trust that we have learned at least some of the lessons that our faithful and earnest preceptors have wished us to master – lessons not always found in textbooks, but suggestive of the life without these scholastic walls which are calling us to action in its busy field. During our stay here, friendship's silver thread has been woven from heart to heart and both teachers and fellow students have become endeared to us, and in years to come, we may look back upon these quiet days spent in study, and be refreshed. Tonight, itself will soon be but a memory; today be yesterday.

In the golden dawn of tomorrow, duty awaits us, and ours will be the honor if we walk in her ways. Vast are the spheres for our labor, vaster our responsibilities. Let us act worthily of our day, not lying down in ignoble, but acting a brave part in lifting heavenward our fellowmen.

> "Build thee more stately mansions, O my Soul.
> As the swift, seasons roll!
> Leave they low-vaulted past!
> Let each new temple, nobler than the last,
> Shut thee from heaven with a dome more fast,
> Till thou at length are free,
> Leaving thine outgrown shell by life unresting sea!"

Mabel Isabel Dove
May 24, 1900.

Commentary

January 1979

For my daughter.

Dear Tanya Maria Robertson: Chattanooga Normal University

Your maternal grandmother graduated June 8, 1900, on a Friday evening – Biology major, music minor. The original of this – along with some other papers – is all fragile and yellowed with age, very delicate. One evening recently, I had an inner push to look in an old box. There I found papers never seen by anyone in the family. Now I've moved, cleaned out desks, boxes, packed, unpacked, filed, sorted many, many times during the years. How these got here or how I came by them is truly weird to me. I was upset and thrilled. The papers have old beloved valuations on them taking me very far back in my time. As I said, no one in the family ever knew of their existence, not even Marjorie. Teleportation? Who knows? I don't. She has been much on my mind this past year, but then one does remember beloved parents and loved ones.

Anyway, put this copy away in your family archives. If I am successful in locating someone who successfully reproduces old papers, all will receive a copy of the original.

Her humanitarianism and idealism are evident, her concern for people. How remarkable to see her belief in reincarnation in her selection of a section of the poem, "The Chambered Nautilus" for her closing.

Your grandfather (John) Bernard Gibbs always said she was years ahead of her time, but I was a child and had no concept of what he meant.

Love,

Mother (Catherine Dove Gibbs)

PART III

THE POEMS OF
MABEL ISABEL DOVE

Original

After looking in the dictionary,

I think I should simply call the following "some lines that rhyme."

For I do not presume to claim that these are a poetry

I only felt the urge to express myself in rhymes,

wishing they might be good,

but knowing full well they are not.

A Confession

This awful junk isn't worth reading,

I know it, but yet I will write.

I 'spose I just set my mouth going

And forget, then, to turn it off tight.

M.D.G.

To Our Son

'Twas it yesterday, (ah, but it seems so long?
How quickly life's sands do run!)
That my heart sang a new and poignant song,
When my arms first enfold my son.

He was given to us – as an answer to prayer,
How deeply our hearts did rejoice!
And we prayed the Lord's way he would help to prepare
A new "John", called to be a new "voice".

This the vision we held: and through fast changing years,
How sweetly the budding life grew!
And through bungling we tried, mid our hopes and our fears,
To the vision and task to be true.

How we love him, what joy he has given our hearts!
How strong, clean, and true is his youth.
The "one thing thou lackest," He only imparts,
Who the way is, the life, and the truth.

Oh, my Son, in life pathways are pitfalls and sands,
And many a storm and fierce shocks.
But there's One offers you a foundation that stands,
Take it now– build your life on that Rock.

M.D.G.

When's She Comin'?

The little boys,
Their charming noise,
Are daily much indulging,
The while to help them big to your
Their tummies' fats are bulging.

The mommies dear,
And daddies cheer
Make life well worth the living,
While each one does the best he can,
To others gladly giving.

I want to see
My dear babee.
Please tell me when she's comin',
And if I know when she was due,
I'd surely come a-runnin'!

My best love and kisses
To the sweetheart of misses.
From your fond, loving mother.
(And you'll ne'er another!)

M.D.G.

Pome

The family liked the little gifts
And Dove thought it was dandy,
That Marjorie sent to Doug and him,
That good salt-water candy.

I hope someday that you will come
To see us in our home,
And when you do, I promise, not
To bore you with a "pome."

M.D.G.

A So-called "Poem" for Darling Kay

This is a so-called "poem" that I wrote,
But don't let that alarm you.
It isn't suitable to quote —
Don't say I didn't warn you!

Darling Kay:

I loved those days you spent at home
They meant so much to me!
How liltingly talk flowed along
From grave to repartee!

And more I learned to value you,
And know your worth so true-
My heart feels gratitude to God,
That He has lent me you.

I think of all the thought and care,
The prayers that rose for you
The hopes and fears that gave at length,
Their place to faith that grew

Your father dear is with us still,
In heaven for us he prays,
And what he left, his faith in God
We'll treasure all our days!

I think that in a special way,
His work goes on in you.
God grant you'll bear the flaming torch,
As he would have you do!

I think, in Christ, he's by our side,
And smiles encouragement,
Reminds us, "Heaven's our Home."
It's richer since he went.

M.D.G.

To My First Granddaughter, November 8, 1946

Ah, so you have come, what a glad happy day!
Although you were just a bit early.
I rejoice that you are here, and I'm hoping your eyes
Will be blue and your hair curly.

But hair curly or straight, eyes brown, green or blue
You are welcome, most welcome to me.
And your hair is just right whatever the hue.
And your eyes, too, as long as they are.

Your family's agog, from small David to Gram.
And you grandpa Sam, too, when I phoned.

Lesley M.   Fri 4 pm

Dink said it was great, would tell it to Dad–
In fact, we're all feeling high toned.

You see, we've been wishing and looking for you.
At your coming, our hearts are expanding
And now it's almost too good to be true,
That, at last, you have made a happy landing.

And now (to change the figures) that your ship is launched
well I trust that your mates you will be hailing,
That for you and your Mummy and Daddy, all three
There will be lots of fun and smooth sailing.

I'm awfully anxious to find out the name
Of the hospital where you first cried
The monikers also be which you are called
By those friends of yours since you arrived.

For its wanting to put in the paper I am

That each person that knows us to see
And understand clearly the why of the grin.
That is spread over the glad face of me.

M.D.G.

To Kay, 1949

Dear, that was a wonderful letter,
It was —well it couldn't be better.
Made me smile, laugh, and sigh,
Think of days long gone by ---
And it made me most deeply your debtor.

I'm sorry to miss the great pleasure,
I'd love having you here, without measure,
If "three days" will seem
A boom to be hailed as a treasure.

So, come, tho' for shorter or longer,
For, too, are you, I'm surely "a longer".
When you come, I'll be glad,
When you go, I'll be sad —
For my love for you daily grows stronger.

Now if this awful "poem" should slay you,
Stay back, for the law's on your side,
For killing a thing so atrocious,
Is a "home side" well justified?

M.D.G.

Dearest Kay, So Far Away But Always Gay
July 19, 1950

I said, "Today
I'll write to Kay,
For I owe her a letter
Then, when I write, she'll owe me one,
And I will like that better."

So here's a start.
At least in part.
Now first, I'd be a knowin'
Just how my gal's a-comin' on,
And how are thing a-goin'?

If you are sick,
Just tell me quick.
Look, Kitten, don't you stall!
If it be Flu or Polio,
Come now, my dear, "Tell all."

My Mommie kind,
Said, "Children, mind,
Keep always in the pink.
For when you do, you never have
Ole nasty stuff to drink."

But if one day,
A germ should stay,
Just nip it in the bud,
And like a bomb that wouldn't work,
T'will fall just like a dud.

I wish that I
Might wander by
And tea with you imbibe
But you're so far, I cannot see
Nor gather all my tribe

I hope, 'fore long
A day will dawn,
I'll find more to my liking
When I shall have my children all
By limousine or biking

I 'spose that you
Want what I do
To you I'll be revealing.
Well, here it is: good health at length
Is all my migraines healing

And over me,
The families,
Kind watch is ever keeping,
And which Dave spends a week at camp,
A peace is o'er us creeping

The little boys,

Their charming noise,
Are daily much indulging,
The while to help them big to grow,
Their tummies fat are bulging

And Mommie dear,
And Dad's good cheer
Make life well worth the living.
While each one does the best he can —
To others gladly giving

I want to see
My dear babe
Please tell me when she's comin',
And if I know when she was due,
I sure would come a-runnin'!

My best love and kisses
To the sweetest of Misses,
From your fond, loving Mother.
(You will ne'er have another!)

M.D.G.

A Bread and Butter Letter to Louise

On my visit, September 15-20, 1950

Dear Friends of the Nicklin Gaston Tribe,
I pray you bend an ear
To these good wishes that I send
Health, happiness, good cheer!

I wish that I could fully tell
How I enjoyed those days!
I'm sending you most cordial thanks
And singing yet, your praise.

I still enjoy, as I recall,
And live the hours again,
And when you're famous, I shall say,
"I knew them, way back when."

Those darlings, little blue-eyed Jane,
And brown-eyed Doris, too.
They put their heads together, then
Surprising things they do!

When Marjorie, in her clear, sweet voice,
At evening "service" sings,
I dream of what the years may hold
Of good and splendid things.

John makes me think of Knights of Old,
(But minus swords and lances).
With thoughtful acts of courtesy,
Our pleasure he enhances.

Then Mimi comes in hopefully,

As such a Mother can
I'm sure she must be pleased as Punch,
With such a gifted clan.

For Geraldine with quiet grace,
Presides wherever needed,
And is a daughter's model, who
Is being aptly heeded.

I hope that at some future time,
I may a rain check claim
On Bobbie's kindly promises,
And hear him play again.

And you, my dear, you fill your place, find
At home, and school, and church.
I'll ne'er find one except you, though
Through all the worlds I search.

It's good to see my folks again,
It makes me stop and ponder,
If it be true, as has been said,
That absence makes us fonder.

And so, Arron we lay aside.
Each clamant, busy care,
And body, mind, and soul renew,
In rest and vital prayer
OR
And so we turn aside and rest
In holy quietness,
While with His own creative power,
He comes our souls to bless.

M.D.G.

A Thank You Note to My Dear Catherine

For the radio she sent on June 13, 1950 – my birthday

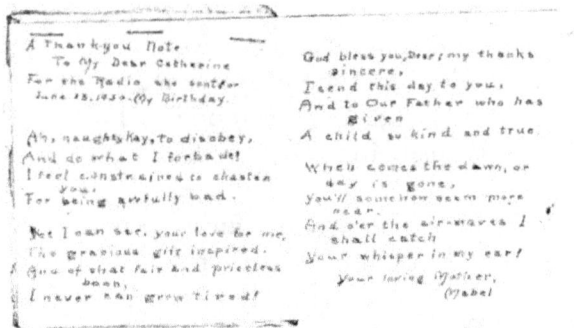

Ah, naughty Kay, to disobey,
And do what I forbade!
I feel constrained to chasten
For you being awfully bad

Yet I can see, your love for me,
The gracious gift inspired.
And of that fair and priceless boon,
I never can grow tired!

God bless you, Dear; my thanks sincere,
I send this day to you,
And to Our Father who has given
A child so kind and true

When comes the dawn, or day is gone,
You'll somehow seem more near,
And o'er the air waves I shall catch
Your whisper in my ear!

Your loving Mother,
M.D.G.

Lula, 1950

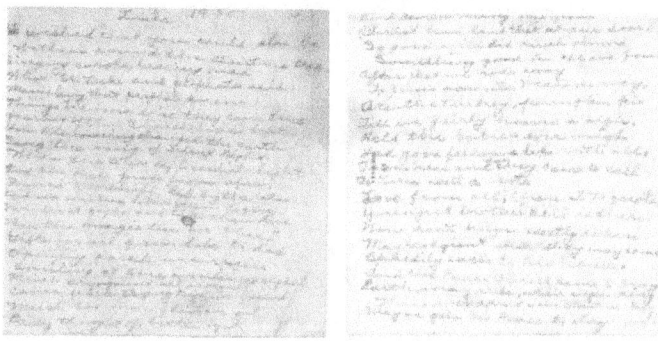

We wished that you could alas be
With us round the Christmas tree
Singing carols, hearing read
What St. Luke and prophets said.

Marveling that prophets knew
Things to come e'er they came true
Hearing of the Christ child's birth
How his coming changed the earth

Sang the song of silent night
When the start diffused its light
And the noise hum from afar
Found the child led by the star

And we wished like them to give
Our best gifts and like them live,
Then the magic tree we "had" —
Gifts for all from the babe to dad

Opening parcels in surprise
Smiling at the wondering eyes
Much enjoyment all around
Came from crying toys we found
Much too many did we get

Being thought of, better yet.
And remembering the good
(Christ had laid that at our door)

So good will did much abound
Something good in sleave found
After that we rode away
To Jesus' parents, Westerner way,

At the turkey, pumpkin pie
Till we fairly heaved a sigh,
Held the babies ever nigh
Had good fellowship with all
To our near and far they came to call

To Korea sent a note
Love, from all (from it to quote)
Youngest brother Bill is there,
Now don't know exactly where

May God grant that they may come
Steadily each to his home
And the Peace Christ came to bring
Earth may rule while angels sing

This was spent our Christmas Day
May we gain his Peace to stay.

M.D.G.

To My Dearest Kay on Saint Valentine's Day
February 14, 1951

I have a brown-eyed lassie,
That I should love to see
But many a mile doth intervene,
And she is far from me

But though it grieves me sorely
That we're so far apart,
Miles cannot really separate —
She lives within my heart!

For there's a place beloved
At which we daily meet,
and find our hearts united
At God's blest Mercy Seat!

This is a song my mother sang when I was a little girl,
Slightly altered to fit the occasion.

"Oh, who is the queen of the roses,
Gardener can you say?
The queen of the roses to me, sir,
Is my own dear daughter Kay.

The rose is the queen,
Yes, the queen of the flowers,
But Kay is the queen,
Yes, Kay is the queen of the roses!"

M.D.G.

My Dream of Kay, March 31, 1952

My Dream of Kay
Last night I had a lovely dream,
I dreamed, dear Love, of you!
So real and natural did it seem,
I thought it must be true.

When to the faucet I had gone,
My water jar to fill,
I saw a coat, dark green and long —
And then I stood stock still.

And as I stood a-pondering
On whose the coat might be,
With all my wits a-wandering —
You came and stood by me!

Oh, what a joy and what a thrill,
And what a big surprise!
Till realism put a chill
Into your glowing eyes.

This was a dream I'd love to keep,
Safe hidden in my heart,
Then I could see you in my sleep,
Tho we were far apart.

The dream has brought so much of cheer,
I wish that it might stay.
I wish you'd really soon be here.
And never go away!

Your loving Mother
-M-
Mar. 31, 1952.

Last night I had a lovely dream,
I dreamed, dear Love, of you!
So real and natural did it seem,
I thought I must be true.

When to the faucet I had gone,
My water jar to fill,
I saw a coat, dark green and long –
And then I stood stock still.

And as I stood a-pondering
On whose the coat might be,
With all my wits a-wondering –
You came and stood by me!

68

Oh, what a joy and what a thrill,
And what a big surprise!
Till realism put a chill
Into your glowing eyes.

This was a dream I'd love to keep
Safe hidden in my heart.
Then I could see you in my sleep,
Tho we were far apart.

The dream has brought so much of cheer
I wish that it might stay.
I wish you'd really soon be here
And never go away!

Your loving mother,

M.D.G.

A Gift From Kay, June 12, 1952

"What a lovely birthday box!
It's from my kiddie Kay;
I'll just put it aside, right now,
And open on "B" day."

But when I had inspected it,
And wondered what was in it,
I "'cided" then, (as Douglas says)
I couldn't wait a minute.

But quickly tore the wrappings off,
And there to me revealed,
Were two attractive, nifty tags
The box before concealed.

At once I donned the "fig leaves" gay
And saw slight alteration
Would make them fit me now, today
And future generations!

They came in just nick of time,
For on this very morning,
I gave many some, grown too short
To serve for my adorning.

I thank you heartily love,
That you remembered me,
Sent feathers for your lovely dove,
So beautiful to see!

Lots of love,
M.D.G.

A Proud Grandmother, February 2, 1954

One happy day, some years ago,
(It was on ground-hog day,
If he saw his shadow, I do not know)
A babe came with us to stay!

Her hair was dark as her father's was
As he held her close in his arms,
He smiled in blissful joy because
He was under the spell of her charms.

In mutual joy we watched her grow,
A little bit every year,
Till she passed by mine and I reached below
The lowest tip of her ear.

And ever since in worth of lights,
She through the years has grown,
Until today, a happy wide,
She has children of her own.

It came about at the self-same time,
But going with the other,
That I became — my eyes did shine —
A happy, proud grandmother!

M.D.G.

Kay's Visit, April 1955

My very littlest girl
Came home to make a visit,
I didn't make a curl
For her! How odd, but is it?

For I was sick in bed,
Scarce able to be up
With weakly bended head
That sipped milk from a cup.

But when she hove in sight,
'Twas like a sunny ray,
That made the whole sky bright
Upon a happy day!

For I began to laugh
('Twas she herself asked for it)
Just like a silly calf
I can't guess how she bore it!

But she, poor thing, did manage
In fact, she joined the fun
It gave us the advantage,
Felt better, everyone.

I had the grandest time
Her visit was a boon.
In every way just prime!
But it ended far too soon.

I still just love my night gown
So dainty and so pretty,
None sweeter found in big town
Nor even in the city.

But memories will last
Our good times long will linger
And minds bring up the past,
Though stirred by even a finger.

Hope soon you'll come again,
And bring sweet Mim along.
You'll think you hear "Big Ben"
So big our welcome song.

M.D.G.

When The Youngest One Came Home, August 1956

How glad we were that summer's day,
When the youngest one came home!
But farewell's quite the other way
When parting is to roam.

But oh! The good times in between,
We never shall forget
Their memory and what they mean
All lingers with us yet

And then the swiftly passing years,
If we must be apart,
We'll cherish them and all that cheers
Held fast within the heart!

This is my heart felt deep desire:
Come oftener and stay longer
Chicago's mood is not so dire,
But I've a mighty "hanger!" (for you)

M.D.G.

The Swift Passing Years

The passing years go hastening only
And naughty can check their pace,
Tho' ought we wish life's reckoning
Might grant a day of grace.

We count each New Year birthday as gift,
A treasure to invest,
That rich returns to god and man
May come from our bequest.

Within my heart a prayer I make,
To use each shining hour,
In ways the rivers direct,
And daily shall empower.

For you this year and all the years,
This is my deep desire.
That life be blest with happiness,
He only can inspire.

M.D.G.

To Louise, On Her Birthday

Just now I heard a rumor
Your birthday's very near!
So here are my best wishes
For a bright and happy prosperous year!

But better than good wishes,
I pray and earnest prayers,
That more and more His Presence
Will make life sweet and fair.

When ways seen dark, uncertain,
Perplexed, you feel unsure,
Relining on His guidance,
Your heart may rest in secure.

You know so well His friendship,
You've proved Him in the past.
May trust each day grow sweeter
And deeper than the last.

And as you've scattered sunshine,
Revealed gods skies as blue,
May you continue blessing,
By what you are and so.

M.D.G.

To John, On His birthday, April 3, 1946

Another year has slipped away.
Again, your birthdays here,
Reminding me at length again,
Of one I hold most dear.

What joys and hopes we saw within
Your tiny baby hand,
What life you shed within our hearts,
Not seen on sea or land!

How wonderful to see that you
In height and wisdom grew.
To see that more than mischief could
That roguish mind imbibe.

What hopes and dreams and plans we had
For what your life might hold.
What prayers that we might not constrain
Your choice, but gently mold.

Your father longed that you might take
The torch when his hand failed.
I would have missed from out my life
That's been a special treat.

And I am truly grateful,
That you have come my ways,
Your friendship means so much to me
I'd love to have you stay!

If someone who has magic,
His "wishing well" could lend
I'd wish our love might grow right on,
And never, Never, end.

May all your skies grow brighter,
With every year I Pray.
Like paths of just men shining more.
Unto the Perfect Day!

M.D.G.

Ethel's Birthday, May 23, 1946

So, one of these "can't get around it's"
Has come to my Ethel again!
A "must be" in every mans' language living.
So we bear it, and sometimes we grin.

All the same we're chagrined that time's foot prints
So plainly on us can be seen,
And we try to outwit the old tyrant.
But he knows all the tricks – he's that keen!

Yes, we grin as our vision turns backward,
And we see what we got with the years.
Love, friendship, and work, baby fingers.
Joy, grief, – but more gladness than tears.

And a warm wave of thankfulness fills us.
So much has been ours, and still is.
And we long to give of our fullness –
For the gifts and the blessing are His.

Now one of the gifts that I treasure,
Is the friendship of someone like you.
It is something that often been tested.
And always found faithful and true.

So, this is my prayer for your birthday.
May this year and all others be bright.
As with sure, growing sense of His presence.
You serenely advance toward the light.

M.D.G.

On Julie's Birthday, October 15, 1946

The days of the years of my life —
To go deep into that, is it best?
Except a glance back and one forward in faith.
And then on today, where it rests.

I wish that today and all others.
Good health and contentment you'll know.
And devotion on love to the Father above,
And to all you may see help here below.

So, I say "Happy Birthday" to you,
And a "Thank you" to God that you came.
For you brought us great joy (with a Little alloy)
And you brought to our Hearts a new Flame.

Now I pray that the days out ahead
May bring joy and fulfillment to you,
That your life may expand in heart and in hand,
With the happiness doubled - for two!

M.D.G.

To My Dearest Kay, September 19, 1947

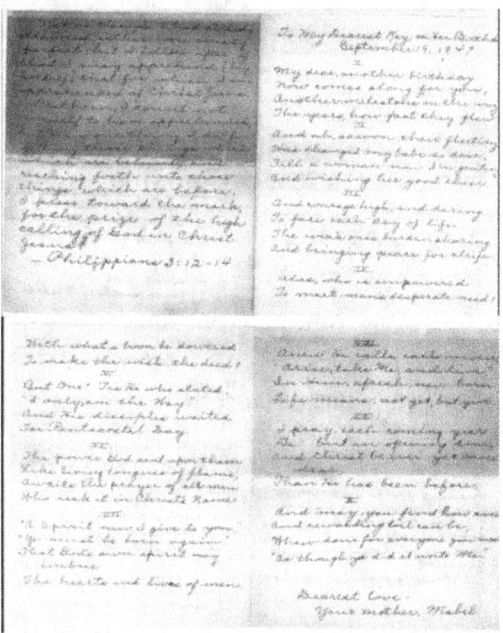

Not as though I had already attained, either were already perfect; but I follow after, if that I may apprehend [lay hold of] that for which I am apprehended by Christ Jesus.

Brethren, I count not myself to have apprehended, but this one thing I do, forgetting those things which are behind, and reaching forth unto those things which are before, I press toward the mark for the prize of the high calling of God in Christ Jesus.
Philippians 3:12-14

My dear, another birthday
Now comes along for you,
Another milestone on the way
The years, how fast they flew

And ah, so soon their fleeting
Has changed my babe so dear,
Till a woman now I'm greeting
And wishing her good cheer.

And courage high, and daring
To face each day of life.
The weak one's burden sharing.
And bringing peace for strife.

Alas, who is empowered
To meet man's desperate need?
With what a boon be dowered
To make the wish, the deed?

But one! 'Tis He who stated,
"I, only, am the Way."
And His disciples waited
For Pentecostal Day.

The power God sent upon them
Like living tongues of flame,
Awaits the prayer of all men
Who seek it in Christ's name.

"A spirit new I give to you,"
"Ye must be born again."
That God's own spirit may imbue
The hearts and lives of men.

Anew He calls each man.
"Arise, take Me, and live."
In Him, afresh new-born
Life means, not get, but give.

I pray, each coming year
Be but an opening door,

And Christ be even yet more dear,
Than He has been before.

And may you find how sweet
And rewarding toil can be,
When done for everyone you meet
"As though ye did it unto me."

M.D.G.

To My Dearest Catherine On Her Birthday
September 19, 1948

Another anniversary's here
Of the day you came to town.
They speed up faster every year –
But smile, no use to frown!

If years could only come and go
And never take their toll,
We think we'd like to have it so,
But life hands out no dole

We pay for everything we get
And even what we don't
What we don't but with toil and sweat
We lose because we won't

Although some good must pass away,
More good the years may give,
If we the price will freely pay
And nobly strive and live

I pray the best along life's way
Be yours in richest store,
To walk and serve and love each day
With God forevermore!

If a lovely good fairy would just come along
And say I could have but three wishes
I'd wish to see you, and sing the old Birthday song
And have dinner with your favorite dishes

Then, of course, there's the paddling I'd just have to give
So your goodness and growth would not tarry
And one for each year you're permitted to live,
And a good one on which you're to marry!

Tho the flowers of earth fade all soon
We shall fin them in heaven in deathless bloom.

M.D.G.

On Jewel's Birthday, 1949

It doesn't matter what we do,
When birthdays come hoppin',
There's always one to follow each,
And nothing seems to stop them.

You may as well take my advice,
I know just what it's like,
When birthdays come and pass on by,
While going down the pike.

Just welcome each one with a grin,
There's something good they're givin'
In fact, when we've no more of 'em
Life won't be worth the living.

When finally, the years have passed,
And there's no more to borrow,
How fine it will be, if first and last,
We gave more joy than sorrow!

M.D.G.

To My Own Precious Little Girl On Her "Grown-up" Birthday

I tried to find a lovely card
To help me to express
The lovely things I wish for you
That all your life may bless.

But nothing sounds quite good enough
To say the prayers I make for you
It's wide and deep and long as life
Like here and life a-new
"life is a fragment of Eternity."

May the joy you've given others,
In your ever thoughtful way
Return to you a hundredfold
On this very Happy Birthday.

M.D.G.

A Day to Remember, September 19, 1950

Do you know the theme of my discourse
This fair September morn?
Yes, it commemorated the day
On which my Kay was born

You were a little fairy babe,
So tiny and so sweet,
I thanked the Father that you came,
And made my joy complete!

When first you nursed, your eyes popped wide,
As if you'd heard from home,
And liked your present place so well,
That you'd no farther roam

I'm glad you stayed; you made the world
A lovelier place for me,
And added just the element
For more variety!

My inmost heart sends forth a prayer —
A Happy Birthday Dear,
And may God guide you all the way
Along a happy year!

Love from your mother,

M.D.G.

To My One and Only Little Granddaughter,

Leota Catherine Friend

On her 4th birthday, November 8, 1950

Accompanying a red wool pleated skirt
with shoulder straps and a front-fastened
White blouse, edged with red-flowered ruffles
On the collar and short sleeves, and part way down the front.

I know a little secret,
D'you think that you can guess?
It's about a certain package,
That holds a little-----.

It's coming to remind you
That on a special day,
You stopped with special people
Who wanted you to stay.

It says that---------loves you,
And helps to celebrate'
By sending Birthday Greetings
To you, November eight.

So won't you put it on you,
And have your picture made?
I will serve until we see you--
Please don't be long delayed!

M.D.G.

To Louise on Her Birthday, November 14, 1950

For Christmas, or when you are ill,
I've cards on hand the need to fill,
But on your birthday, I must sing,
My own wee song, my wish to bring.

I'd like to wish the bluest skies
Would follow after each sunrise,
Heigh ho! Another box of that delicious candy?
You know, or do you want, it surely is a day

A gracious way to greet,
And put across a wish,
It leaves a memory sweet--
It really is some dish!

How nice that Christmas brings
Kind thoughts and deeds that meet
In royal folk like Kings--
Thanks for your royal treat!!

M.D.G.

A Birthday Letter, September 20, 1951

Whatever am I doing
That it sneaked up on me!
Why only yesterday I shopped
To find what I could see

Of something that would be just right
For this your n'th birthday.
Then later send it on to you--
But I lost a week some way!

In other words, your birthday
Stole unawares on us.
We didn't know it till today
That we had "missed the bus".

We're terribly chagrined,
My worry will not hush --
That I could do a thing like that
To one I love so much!

But I'm sure you understand,
Have done the same yourself?

I helped a little canning fruit
To place upon the shelf.

A letter long since started
Said, "Tell what I can send
To dear Kay G. for her birthday —
Pray your assistance lend."

Well, take this check and purchase
Something from me to you
You know just what you want — I don't.
Though late, perhaps 'twill do.

To help you to remember
(Of all the things I say)
I love you now and always,
In just the same old way.

And best of all, He's with us
If we will have it so,
And will be, always, every day,
Wherever we may go!

Dearest love,

M.D.G.

To Kay, On Her Birthday, September 19, 1954

[handwritten manuscript reproduction of the poem]

I was thinking just the other day
About my littlest daughter Kay –
That on the nineteenth of September
Will come a day I'll e'er remember.

That happy day I'll ne'er forget
Nor its recurrence e'er regret,
Because it brought my littlest daughter
I'm very happy that I "bought" her.

I wish for her a Happy Birthday
And every joy that comes this earth way.
That God her days will all imbue
With happiness enough for two!

And may it happen more and more
She'll bring us joy just as she did of yore,
And be a witness for our King,
And help His reign of love to bring!

M.D.G.

You're going to have an awful lot of happiness today.
There's going to be a lot of things.
Turn out your favorite way!
There's going to be bright days ahead.
Brim full of dreams come true.
If only HALF my happy hopes are realized for you!

Your loving mother,

M.D.G.

To Kay on Her Birthday, September 19, 1956

Do you know what's today in your age?
Well I didn't myself, right away
For the kids had torn off the calendar page,
That carries the meaningful day.

And I'm sorry as sorry can be,
You're not getting this letter just now
Instead my writing for you to see,
What my feelings desire to vow.

But my "forgetter" is so very good,
And my "rememberer" so bad,
That often when I wish that I could,
I find that I can't and am sad.

But this thing I shall ne'er forget
Where e'er I roam, on land or sea
That you are my own darling pet,
And dear beyond all words to me!

Your loving Mother,

M.D.G

97

The Tale of the Check

Within his little envelop
A shirt and blouse are hidden;
You say for that you cannot hope,
And think I'm just kidding!

But if you'll take a little sip,
This little envelope may house,
You may exchange it if you wish
For a natty shirt and blouse.

M.D.G.

Our Young Damsel

Ah, here was a technique
Not easy to match.
And yes, one must admire
The ease and dispatch

With which our young damsel
Had made her debut,
A rare "first appearance"
And quite "impromptu".

And she was e'er moted,
Until she was grown,
For original trends
Distinctly her own.

So, its happed by the persons
Who hold her most dear,
She'll continue the pattern
She set yesteryear.

What patterns of "ease and dispatch"!

M.D.G.

<u>*Mother's Garden*</u>

Soon after the death of my dear mother, Julia McCluer Dove,
September 19,1927

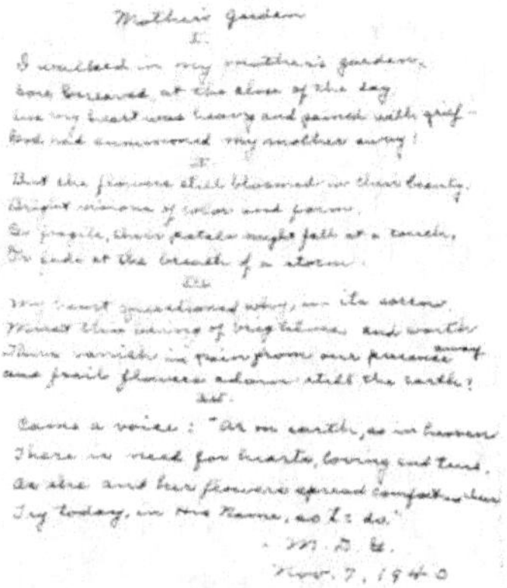

I walked in my Mother's garden,
Sore bereaved, at the close of the day.
And my heart was heavy and pained with grief-
God had summoned my mother away!

But the flowers still bloomed in cheer beauty,
Bright visions of color and form.
So fragile their petals might fall at a touch,
Or fade at the breath of a storm.

My heart questioned why, in its sorrow,
Must this being of brightness and worth
Thus vanish in pain from our presence away,
And frail flowers adorn still the earth?

Came a voice: "As on earth, so in Heaven,
There is need for hearts, loving and true.
As she and her flowers spread comfort and cheer
Try today, in His name, so to do."

M.D.G.

Mother's Day, December 1, 1951

Did you know that Mother's day
Is the first day of December?
Oh, you thought it came in May?
Oh, I know, for I remember!

For to Jim, likewise to me,
It's the birthday of our mothers,
And 'twill not forgotten be,
For it's different from all others

In her honor, you, I greet
And I send to you this token,
I would lay at her dear feet
Of the tie that now is broken.

And I pray that all things good,
Every day will come to you
All His love, that's by you stood
Live in you the whole year through!

M.D.G.

The Joy of Motherhood, November 1, 1953

I've
How lovely and how fair was she,
That day I saw her stand,
With inner light not found on sea
Or ever on the land.

The joy of coming motherhood
She felt within heart,
It made her long for all that's good –
Did happiness impart.

It glowed with beauty in her face
In gentle looks and mild,
Imbuing them with added grace
As of a lovely child.

How gracious is God's wondrous plan
That lets us work with Him,
To bring choice happiness to man
Fills life up to the brim!

M.D.G.

To My Dear Kay on Father's Day, June 17, 1951

I am thinking as doubtless you're thinking
Of our loved one, your father so dear.
For deep in our hearts we still hold him,
Though parted for many a year.

As Father's Day brings to remembrance,
How deeply we loved, and still love,
We know he is ours, will be always,
God keeps him for us, up above.

Today we would honor his memory,
Would lay more than words at his feet.
Life lived the way he lived it,
Would make our high tribute complete!

With love,

M.D.G.

Father's Day, June 17, 1956

In memory of our dear Father

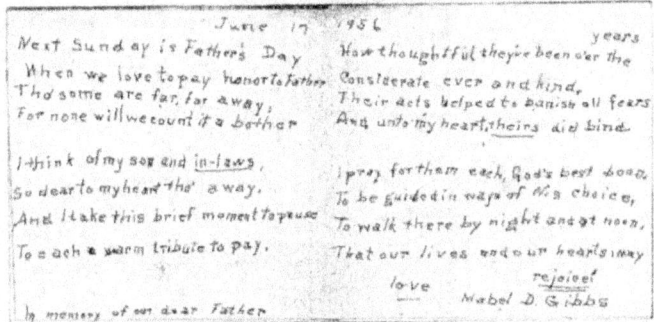

Next Sunday is Father's Day
When we love to pay honor to Father
Though some are far, far away,
For none will we count it a bother

I think of my son and in-laws,
So dear to my heart tho' away,
And I take this brief moment to pause,
To each a warm tribute to pay.

How thoughtful they've been o'er the years
Considerate ever and kind,
Their acts helped to banish all fears,
And unto my heart, theirs did bind.

I pray for them each, God's best boon
To be guided in ways of His choice,
To walk there by night and at noon,
That our lives and our hearts may rejoice!

Love,

M.D.G.

A Valentine - To My Dear Friends

Upon this special day of fate,
A Valentine I send
But tho' any day's a splendid date
To think of each dear friend.

Because I want you all to know,
At least a little part
Of what will ever live and grow
For you within my heart.

Please tell that Darling Baby mine,
And Bill so brave and bold,
I want you for my Valentine,
To love and have and hold.

I know a friendly little man
Who is very fat and jolly,
Who likes to come round if he can
With mistletoe and holly.

M.D.G.

A Valentine to John and Eve

In honor of this day of fate,
Although it is a little late,
I send a valentine,
On this, or any other day,
My heart for you both pine!

And this what I want to say,
My daughter and my son,
Pray be my valentine today,
I think it would be such fun!

For if your love for me is great
As is my love for you,
There is no knife that soon or late,
Can cut our love in two.

M.D.G.

Valentine

How good it was to hear from you,
In that nice little letter
I'm looking soon
To go out and that is better.

Did the little bird fly from the wood,
Upon the Valentine?
It all did me a lot of good,
It seemed to me just fine!

M.D.G.

A Late Valentines Letter, 1951

I was sick when I should have been sending
My valentines out in the mail,
Forgive me, I'm awfully sorry —
And this is not just a tall tale

But I thought I wound send them in spite of
The fact that they'd be very late,
If I didn't, you'd be obligated
For almost a whole year to wait.

And anyway, can we be certain
We'll be sending out valentines then?
But if we are not, 'twill be better
Than anything dram of by men!

But early or late, I am sending
A bushel of love, and a peck
And I know if you'll send me a bushel,
That nothing our loving can wreck!

Your Pal,
M.D.G.

Valentine, February 2, 1952

The very nicest valentine
Was sent to us one year,
"From him to her, from her to him" –
Which way was not quite clear.

It really came a bit too soon,
To call a valentine;
In fact, it came on ground–hog day –
For us the sun did shine!

We both maintained our right to "it."
It seems to us so fair;
And since it was marked with no address,
We each one claimed a share.

So things went on in that same way,
For many happy years;
We felt a calm security
That quieted our fears.

And then it happened, as we [feared] thought
Yes, someone came one day,
And spite of all that we could do,
He carried her away.

She seemed a very happy girl,
Desired as much to go,
That when he asked us for her hand,
We could not say them "no."

And as we gave her up to him –

She lived with us no more;
But in the end, we were ahead,
Because that makes us four!

M.D.G.

Be My Valentine, February 14, 1957

Won't you be my valentine
Forever and a day?
For it would surely be just fine
If that could last away.

But I know of a better yet:
Come home and learn his name,
And when you do, you will, I bet,
Be thinking just the same.

M.D.G.

On Christmas Day, December 4 & 5

From Heaven came a little Boy
To look for you and me.
He wanted us to share His joy –
And ever with Him be!

So greatly hath our Father – God hath loved,
He left His home in Heaven,
To live with men, His well-beloved,
And serve them there as leaven.

And so we sing on Christmas Day,
The song the angels sang
Of glory, that shall be for ages
As when the heavens first sang!

So glorious was the Father's love
He gave His only son,
Who came to earth from Heaven above,
With joy for everyone.

And so we sing on Christmas day,
The song the angels sang
With glory, that shall last for age,
As when the heavens first rang!

And so on this merry Christmas day
There out the whole round earth,
We celebrate in some glad way,
The blessed Savior's birth!

M.D.G.

Christmas

Can you hear the joy bells ringing,
And the angel chorus singing?
Through war's clamor and its strife
And it's tragic how of life within

Can we hear the joy bells ringing,
Angels' glad exultant singing?
In those inns, there's no room,
Hearts reject Him, to their doom;

But to those who watch and listen,
Angels sing, the star's a-glisten.
And the blessed angel voice
Comes and bids their hearts rejoice.

For God's promises are sure,
Wrong must fail, the right endure.
May our actions not delay.
But with prayer, speed the day

When all swords shall plowshares be,
Spears a-pruning we shall see.
Lion fellowship with lamb,
God be known in every land.

Naught to injure nor destroy,
Lives be freed from sin's alloy.
Then in truth we'll keep His birth.
Bring good will and peace on earth!

Doing good will and peace on earth,
All hearts know the savior's birth!
Every heart knows Jesus' birth!
Epilogue we shall then hear joy bells sing
Angels' loud, triumphant sing!

M.D.G.

God Needs Your Voice Today

How much God needs your voice today
This day of deep unrest!
To sound clear and fearless note
Which heeding, man is blest.

No lines might break nor gap remain
Unfilled where death assailed.

Ah, where can life's rewards be found.
So high, so ever sure,
As those that come from heart of men
And evermore endure.

How much God needs your voice today.
This day of deep unrest.
To sound a clear and fearless note.
Which heeding man is blest.

M.D.G.

New Life

In Him afresh newborn life means "With joy I give"!

I pray each coming year
May be an opening door.
And Christ be yet more dear
Than He has been before!

M.D.G.

Reflections

It is well to remember whenever we're irked,
By the things that the others may do,
That perhaps they are feeling the very same way,
And that maybe a little shuffled, too.

For this is a truth to be pondered with care:
Since none may perfection attain,
We each with the others should gently forbear,
And from speaking unkindly refrain.

There is no one so fortunate understand the sum,
Who has never a fault to be born,
He who judges another very likely is one
Who also has traits he should mourn.

Alas! Who is empowered
To meet despairing need?
With what a boom be lowered
To make the will, the deed?

But one! Tis he who stated.
"I only am the way,"
And his discipline awaited
For Pentecostal Day!

The Power God went upon them,
Like living tongues of flame,
Awaits the faith of all men
Who seek it in Christ name.

"I give a spirit new"
"Ye must be born again."
That Christ's spirit must imbue,
The very innocent heart lives of men.

Again, anew he calls each morn,
"Arise, take Me and live."

M.D.G.

Angel's Song

When angels sought for listening ears
    To hear their glorious song,
They found them not in crowded ways,
    Among the heedless throng.

But where the shepherds watched their flock,
    In a quiet field by night,
The angel of the Lord came down,
    In heavenly splendor bright.

"Fear not," said he, "To you I bring
    Glad news of Jesus' birth."
"To God be glory," angels sang,
    "Good will and peace on earth!"

Today despite the battle's strife
    And thwarted minds of men,
Lord make each heart a place of peace,
    Where Christ is born again.

Oh, may the song the angels sang,
Yet ever more increase,
Till all the world shall know the love
Of Christ, the Prince of Peace!

M.D.G.

Easter Thoughts, April 17, 1949

Easter Thoughts

The Spring is born!
And each new morn,
Some glad surprise I see;
The bursting bud,
The springing shrub—
From death-how can it be!

From many a bird,
So long unheard,
Bursts forth a joyous song;
Mid sun and showers,
The blooming flowers
Return, tho dead so long.

From out the gloom
Of Jesus' tomb
He comes triumphantly!
His glorious voice
Bids us rejoice,
Now, and eternally.

Lord, I would be
Alive to Thee,
From sin and death set free.
For others live,
And gladly give,
And love victoriously!

— Mabel D. Gibbs

April 17, 1949

The spring is born!
And each new morn,
Some glad surprise I see,
The swelling bud,
The springing shrub,
From death —how can it be!

From many a bird,
So long unheard,
Bursts forth a joyous song,
Mid sun and showers,
The blooming flowers,
Return, tho dead so long.

From out the gloom
Of Jesus' tomb
He comes triumphantly!
His glorious voice
Bids us rejoice,
Now, and eternally.

Lord, I would be
Alive to thee,
From sin and death set free.
For others live.
And gladly give,
And love victoriously!

M.D.G.

Accompany a Tablecloth to John and Eve

March 14, 1949

When gratitude the heart both feel.
For food His goodness sent,
It makes of every common meal
A sacred holy sacrament.

When with his needy ones will share,
Poor out to him war best,
We have enough, and room to spare –
He multiplies the rest.

And when the heart its treasure gives.
To him its purpose binds,
That heart then must completely live,
Life's rich fulfillment finds.

So, when this common cloth you spread,
Upon the common board,
O may you find your souls are fed
With living bread, the Lord!

M.D.G.

Our Gifts, 1949

Over the hills came the Sheppard,
The wise men from lands afar.
They thought in a palace to find him.
But were guided right by a star.

But eagerly all sought the Christ child
And out of their treasure did bring,
What they possessed, rich or humble
But they gave of their best to the King.

Our treasure may be poor and lovely,
As we come at our Saviors behest.
But it is accepted by Jesus,
When to him we are giving our best!

M.D.G.

The Pilgrims, November 19, 1951

In winter's keen and chilling blast,
On a bleak and alien shore,
The pilgrims haven found at last,
Their wanderings were o'er.

Such aspect might appear to some,
Forbidding and austere;
To these from persecution come,
It meant release from fear.

A place they sought to worship God,
With free unfettered mind,
Where, undeterred by tyrant's rod,
Asylum they could find.

What they possessed, they thought will last,
If freedom they might gain;
They rushed their all, nor counted cost,
To break wrong's galling chain.
When they had made safe anchorage,

126

They knelt, and thanks they gave.
Oh cherish well this heritage,
That men have died to save!

Thank God for such courageous souls!
They inspire us on our way,
To choose, with them, the Christ–like goals
And press toward them each day!

M.D.G.

In the Sanctuary

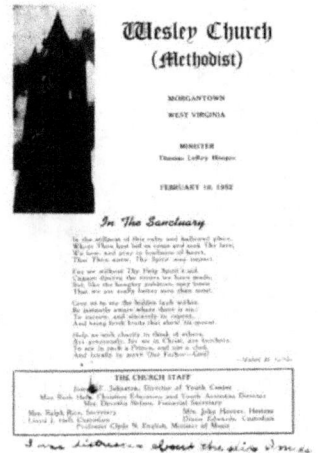

In the stillness of this calm and hallowed place,
Where Thou hast bid us come and seek Thy face,
We bow, and pray in lowliness of heart,
That Thou anew, Thy Spirit may impart.

For we without Thy Holy Spirit's aid,
Cannot discern the errors we have made,
But, like the haughty publican, may boast
That we are really better men than most.

Give us to see the hidden fault within,
Be instantly aware where there is sin;
To sorrow, and sincerely to repent,
And bring forth fruits that show 'tis meant.

Help us with charity to think of others,
Act generously for we in Christ, are brothers;
To see in each a Prince, and not a clod,
And loyally to serve Our Father – God!

M.D.G.

Lenten Thoughts, March 8, 1952

Lenten Thoughts

When e'er I think what woes of heart and mind,
Our Lord once suffered to redeem mankind,
Of how thru love, He drained the bitter cup,
And on the cross of shame was lifted up;

My heart in adoration kneels, with grief
That my iniquities and unbelief
Should be of grievous sorrows such a part
Of all my Savior bore that broke His heart!

And when I learn He chose His life to give,
To pay sin's penalty that man might live,
His purpose thru the ages then I see,
And not a victim slain who could not flee.

Before the earth's foundations yet were laid,
God's plan for man's redemption then was made,
That He should in the flesh seek man, the lost
Altho love's last full measure it must cost

O may I find some self-denying way
A gift to bring, and on the altar lay,
To spread the truth that Christ on Calvary
Has shed His blood to ransom you and me!
—M—

When e'er I think what woes of heart and mind,
The Lord once suffered to redeem mankind;
Of how thru love, He drained the bitter cup,
And on the cross of shame was lifted up.

My heart in adoration kneels with grief
That my iniquities and unbelief
Should be of grievous sorrows such a part
Of all what my Savior bore that broke His heart!

And when I learn He chose His life to give,
To pay sin's penalty that man might live,
His purpose thru the ages then I see,
And not a victim slain who could not flee.

Before the earth's foundations yet were laid,
God's plan for man's redemption then was made.
That He should in the flesh seek man, the lost
Altho love's last full measure it must cost

O may I find some self-denying way
A gift to bring, and on the altar lay,
To spread the truth that Christ on cavalry
He shed His blood to ransom you and me!

M.D.G.

Easter 1953

Ah then my stricken heart with grief is rent,
And marvels at God's grace to mortals sent,
With gratitude profound that such could be
Ordained by God from all Eternity!

Now all the way of Sorrow He has trod,
And here is vindication of our God;
For tho the bitter sting of death He'd borne
Rejoice, He lived again on Easter Morn!

Easter 1953   Mabel D. Gibbs

Ah then my stricken heart with grief is rent,
And marvels at God's grace to mortals sent,
With gratitude profound that such could be
Ordained by God from all Eternity!

Now all the way of sorrow He has trod,
And here is vindication of our God;
For tho the bitter sting of death He'd borne
Rejoice, He lived again on Easter morn!

M.D.G.

Sunday Morning, July 1

Hear the music of the bells,
On a Sunday morning,
For the sound a message tells,
All the air adorning.

"Come to church," they seem to say,
"Come, the bidding heed,
"This is God's own holy day,
"Given to meet our need."

For God's word had bid us, "Come,
"Fail not to assemble,
"Join your brothers, every one
"Make sin's kingdom tremble."

We will haste with willing feet,
To the feast that's spread,
And in fellowship complete,
Take the living bread.

M.D.G.

Courtship

[handwritten draft of the poem below]

A Cherished Reminiscence, a memory fond   you say?
Well here is one: – A man, a mid, a dreamy summer's day.
A ride beyond the city's heart, with kindly chaperone,
A winding mountain road, a jest, a match of merry tune.
A halt beside a sparkling stream, a hunt for flowrets care,
A knightly man, a laughing maid, a wild rose in her hair.
A dainty lunch, then chaperone doth dose, doth take a nap,
The while, with book of poesy, the man and maid chat.
A story told, the birds o'erheard ecstatic music make
As they behold eyes meet, hands clasp, lips-sh!
Chaperone's awake!

M.D.G.

My Wish

There's something fine I wish for you —
Good health and happiness,
Each day linked up with God a new,
And lived with Him to bless!

M.D.G.

The Snowbird

When all de ground with snow is white,
The merry snowbird comes,
And hops about with great delight,
To find de scattered crumbs.

How glad he seems to be to find,
A piece of cake or bread (or)
He wears no shoes upon his feet,
No hat upon his head.

But happiest is he, I know,
Because no rage with bars,
Keeps him from walking on de snow,
And printing it with stars.

M.D.G.

A Memory Letter

[On the back of Memories of Mother]

I share today these thoughts with you,
In this, a memory letter,
I wish you had been privileged
To know (your grandma) my mother better!

M.D.G.

The Beach

I walked along the beach today
And found a lovely shell
Scratched
By sun and
Sands of time

I, too, am a lovely shell
Hold me close
And you will hear
The Ocean roar.

M.D.G.

Cast Away

One I love, two I love,
three I love they say,
four I love, and five I love,
and six I have cast away.

Counting Daisies is not the way,
a lovers love to find,
for the very one I cast aside,
was the one I longed to find.

M.D.G.

Frost Pictures

One cool and frosty morning,
I rose the day to great,
And saw, the roofs adorning,
The prints of fairy feet.

Or, maybe 'twas the tracing
Of fairy fingers drift,
A dainty interlacing
Of tapestry they left.

I pet my heart a glowing,
('twas exquisitely fair!)
In swift response out_ going
To loveliness so rare!

Oh frosty fairy, effin' fingers,
You charm me with your art,
Your fragile beauty fingers,
It's treasured in my heart!

There's surely a Designer
For every least design,
He must be greater finer
Than any form or line.

So, when I view with wonder,
The universe sublime,
I know that over, under,
Still move the Hand Divine!

M.D.G.

Giving Thanks, 1949

Dear Lord, we thank thee for this food,
And for all thy gifts so good.
With Living Bread our spirits feed,
And satisfy our soul's deep need.

As daily we receive Thy care,
Help us with needy, ones to share,
Remembering our Lords decree,
"As ye do to them, ye to Me".

M.D.G.

Life Means to Give

In him a fresh newborn,
Life means "not get, but give!"

I pray each coming year
Mary be an opening door;
And Christ be yet more dear
Than he has been before!

If we are disgruntled as sometimes, we are,
By the things that the others may do,
That perhaps they are feeling the very same way,
And they may be a bit ruffled, too.

For this is a truth the be pondered with care;
Since none may perfection attain,
We each with the other should gently forebear,
And from speaking unkindly refrain.

There is no one so fortunate under the sun,
How has never a fault to be borne.
He who judges another very likely is one.
Who also has traits he must mourn.

Which are behind, and reaching forth unto
Those things which are before, I press toward
The mark for the prize of the high
Calling on God in Christ Jesus."

M.D.G.

Take Heart

The souls that pain and sorrow try,
Though pierced by many a dart,
Are sure there's One who's standing by,
And so again take heart.

M.D.G.

With Thanks

And I was completely surprised:
Quite freely you gave of your service,
But the kindness of heart I most prized.

I wish you might know what your action
Has given of help and good cheer,
Your kindliness I shall remember,
With gratitude many a year.

I thank you again for the favor,
I'd love to return it some way,
I pray that Our Father in Heaven
May bless you and yours every day.

M.D.G.

Another Year Dawning, December 31, 1945

Tomorrow lies before you like
An undiscovered land
With shining possibilities –
The lovely things you've planned

Are blurred into a golden haze
In which you play your past,
In valiant adventures with
A brave and fearless heart

I can do all things through Christ

Another year is dawning
Dear Master, let it be
In working or in waiting
Another year with Thee

M.D.G.

My Tribute

In Response to a Beautiful Letter of Appreciation from my Dear Son John,
August 18, 1950

You cannot know how I was touched
By flowers that you sent.
(That tender message on the card,
To me sure blossom meant.)

I felt the smart of unshed tears,
I thought, "He's giving flowers,
While I their loveliness can see
I'm living conscious hours.

My heart glows warm with gratitude
To God for such a son period.
Rejoices always in his love –
On earth has just begun!

M.D.G.

Trust, Fall 1950

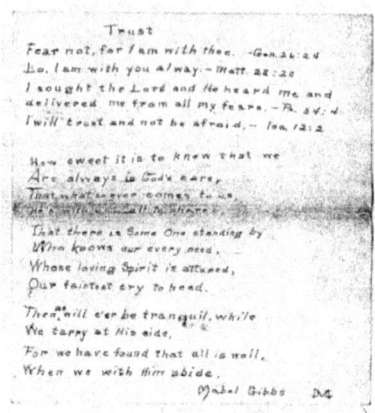

Fear not for I am with thee. Gen. 26:34
Lo, I am with you always. − Matt. 28:20
I will trust and not be afraid. - Isa 12:2
Sought the Lord and He heard me and delivered me from all my fears.
− Ps. 34:4

How sweet it is to know that we
Are always in God's care,
In all that comes of good or ill'
He's present, all to share.

That there is some One standing by
Who knows our every need,
Whose loving Spirit is attuned
Our faintest cry to heed.

Then, we will e'er be tranquil while
We tarry at His side,
For we have found that all is well,
When we with Him abide.

M.D.G.

Trust, Poem Sent to Aunt Lula

Written on a Letter to Kay

How sweet it is to know that we
Are always in God's care,
In all that comes of good or ill'
He's present, all to share.

That there is some One standing by
Who knows our every need,
Whose loving Spirit is attuned
Our faintest cry to heed.

As we meet life's problems harsh,
Our souls He will empower
To come off more than conquerors
In every trying hour

In quietness and confidence,
We'll rest close by His side,
And gain new strength and peace of mind,
As we in Him abide.

M.D.G.

Trust, May 21, 1952

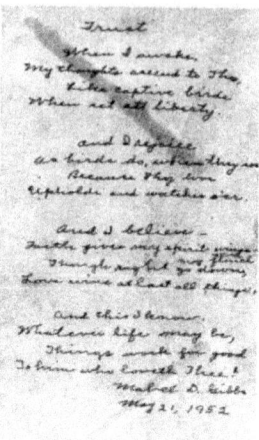

When I awake,
My thoughts ascend to Thee,
Like captive birds
When set at liberty.

And I rejoice
As birds do, when they roar,
Because Thy love
Upholds and watches o'er.

And I believe –
Faith gives my spirit wings.
Though right may wince,
Love wins at last all things.

And this I know,
Whatever life may be,
Things work for good
To him who loveth Thee!

M.D.G.

Trust, May 21, 1952 - Draft

When I awake,
My thoughts arise to thee,
Like captive birds
When set at liberty.

And I rejoice
As birds do, when they roar
Because Thy love
Upholds and watches o'er.

And I believe –
Tho' faith at times may falter
The final triumph
Of right, men cannot alter.

And this I know,
Whatever life may be,
Things work for good
To him who loveth thee!

Or

And I believe
Tho' much I cannot see
Thou it keep in peace
The mind that's stand on Thee

M.D.G.

Give More, December 1955

He like to give a big surprise
And tho' we guess and guess
In spite of very big surmise
We don't have much success.

But one cold day he told me
A certain thing or two,
Just listen and you'll really see
That what I say is true.

But take this little tip from me
And keep it well in mind.
Fresh brew hot fragrant cup of tea
The best that you can find.

Twill warm the cockles of his heart
That thought to him you give
And tho' we do a generous part
Give more and help him live.

M.D.G.

To My Dear Friend Myrtle

So, you had a birthday,
And didn't let me know!
It came upon me unaware,
Oh my, but am I slow!

I'm surely glad you had one,
Your first one, don't you know,
And so I think it's not too late,
To speak and tell you so.

For if you hadn't had one
There's something fine and sweet,
No line might break nor gap remain
Unfilled where death assails.

"Ah, where can life's rewards be found
So high, so ever sure,
As those that come from hearts of men"
And evermore endure.

M.D.G.

Our Pastor, An Appreciation

He is ever the genial friend
Sympathetic and ready to aid,
From his strength and his goodness to spend,
Until his beat part he has played . . .

(Unfinished)

M.D.G.

Brotherhood, 1949

And what is the profit that my can find
To discuss with unkindness another?
I were better by far to rely something kind.
And to act like a loyal true brother.

We all have rough edge, some crude hidden bent,
That may rude other folk the wrong way,
But if always we act with considerate and gracious intent,
We can smooth them–they're just made of clay.

The master has said, "Let the man without sin,
Be the one who cast the first stone."
So, if over folks' fault we are moved to recount,
Let's forget it, remembering our own!

M.D.G.

To Reverend Mr. I. A. Canfield

On his birthday, June 9th, 1954

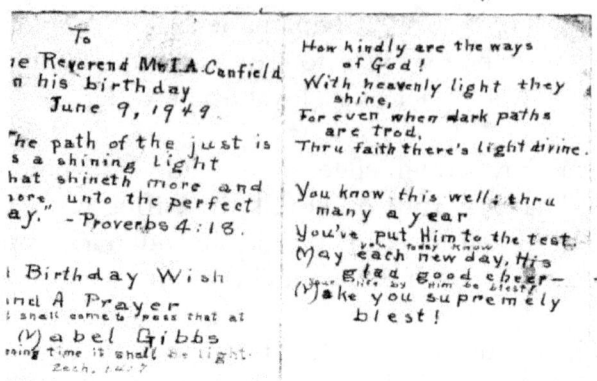

"The path of the just is as a shining light that shineth more
and more unto the perfect day."
- Proverbs 4:18

How kindly are the ways of the God!
With heavenly light they shine.
For even when dark paths are trod,
Thru faith there's light divine.

You know this well; thru many a year
You've put Him to the test
May each new day, His glad good cheer –
Make you supremely blest!

M.D.G.

155

To Dr. Stafford in Cumberland

Who put in my Bridge (teeth) which had come out – for nothing
Dr. Ira H. Stafford, Washington St. Sept 1950 Cumberland, Md.

"There's nothing so kingly as kindness"
Sang one of the poets of old,
I think we could not live without it,
Though our purses might be bulging with gold.

A kindness was shown to me lately,
That not one day were dark and drear,
But each one shining bright and clear.
But too much suns a desert made

No rain means no one's thirst allayed or assuaged
And rainless, man his thirst ne'er slakes,
So, since such wishes can't come true,
I wish you'd keep on being you.

For you can make a dark day bright,
Make heavy burdens seem more light.
Life's waters to the thirsty give,
Who them, reviving, bravely live.

So, I am praying to God instead,
You'll ever share, as now, His Bread,
That His own life within your soul,
May ever help to make men whole.

M.D.G.

Union, November 15, 1953

For in union there is strength
To fulfill our mission,
More effective goals at length
For each town and Christian!

All through the years the church has stood,
Fair or foul the weather,
Forked for freedom, brotherhood
They advanced together!

M.D.G.

To Mrs. Minnie Walters, May 1949

On the accident that broke her arm

Whatever made you go and break
Your strong and husky arm?
You really have too much at stake
To do yourself such harm!

Perhaps in your subconscious mind,
Repressed and out of sight
You may some old frustration find
That now creates this plight.

Maybe you feel an inner urge,
An impulse most terrific,
To carry out some dark design
With action quite specific.

So, see a good psychiatrist,
And psychoanalyze be,
Be if he can't untie your knots,
Just take some bonesi tea!

But putting nonsense all aside,
I sympathize – no fib,
And hope the arm gets well to stay.
One time I break a rib!

But putting nonsense from your eyes,
I really want to say,
With your I deeply sympathize,
Get well to stay and don't delay!

M.D.G.

On a Card to Dr. W. Sproule Boyd

When he collapsed in the pulpit last Sunday, October 22, 1950

Sometimes when crowded is the day
We catch the Master's smile,
And hear His bidding, "Come away
With me and rest awhile."

He knows the limits of our strengths, he knows
And what we can endure,
The needs of mind and body sees
And gain from Him that Peace of Mind
When we with Him abide.

M.D.G.

To Mrs. Clementine Dudderess, May 18, 1954

It's surely good to hear that you are now improving,
We hope the time is near, when you'll toward us be moving.

We love to see you ever, though dismal be the day,
But don't forget , no never, we want you back to stay

We miss you, remember, throughout the bright spring days,
And also in December, For all your kindly ways.

We miss you, we deplore, efficient president,
And pray that soon, once more, with us your time be spent!

So listen to return, they owe no waiting see
For we can't wait to learn how sweet reunions be!

M.D.G.

For Mrs. C. C. Thompson

On the death of her mother, 1947

Ah mother dear, can it be true
That you have gone away?
Your cherished form now lost to view,
And darkened all my day!

Yet then our tears, our thanks we give
That you this long were spared
To show us rightly how to live,
To meet God, be prepared!

But yet my heart will miss you, so —
So close we've been, so long.
You'll not return, but I shall go
To you, and join that throng.

Of loved and lost of other years
Where hearts and voices blend.
And God shall wipe away all tears,

And joy will never end!
But Christ shall be our all in all,
The Lamb, for sinners slain
And we redeemed, no more to fall
With Him for aye shall reign.

But till that glorious day shall come
I want to help some other
Because of all you've meant to me
My precious, sainted mother!

M.D.G.

Comfort

Sent to Mrs. Charles E. Moore and Miss Georgina Smith, on the death of their mother, Mrs. Estello Smith; also to Mrs. G. W. Dudderer on death of her sister, Mrs. Richards; for Mrs. F. Dewy Cornell, August.30, 1950, after her husband was found dead in bed Tuesday morning, August 29, 1950.

Surely he hath born our griefs and earned our powers

In this dark hour of grief,
When love's dear tie you sever,
How comforting the blest belief,
That it is not forever!

For there is One who said,
"He who believes in on me,
Shall live again, thee he be dead
Shall live eternally."

We hear our Savior say
"I never will forsake."
So, though you walk a lonely way,
You'll never be desolate.

163

Then so dry the falling tear,
Our hope is not in vain,
The vanished hand we cherished here,
We'll clasp in heaven again.

By faith our eyes can see,
Our Loved to us restored,
When reunited, we shall be,
Forever with the Lord!

I pray that you may know,
I sympathize with you,
For I have known such comfort, though
My heart was breaking, too.

M.D.G.

When Your Little Boy Went Away, August 23, 1950

On the death of little Douglas Harworth, two-year-old son of Roy and Eleanor Parwall Harworth. He died while being operated on for a brain tumor.

The little life that gave you joy,
Was by the Father lent
Return to Heaven your little boy,
From which he once was sent.

How gracious seems the grievous fate
That dealt this bitter blow;
Yet through the tears and hearts that ache,
By faith God's love we know.

By faith we know that though we part
From our beloved in sorrow,
We'll be united heart to heart
Some happier tomorrow.

And though we cannot understand
Why God your pray denies,
Your darling waits for you in that fair land
For you beyond the skies!

Today I want you both to know
I sympathize with you,
For I have known such comfort, though
My heart was aching, too!

M.D.G.

To Mary Virginia, October 10, 1950

On the death of her parents

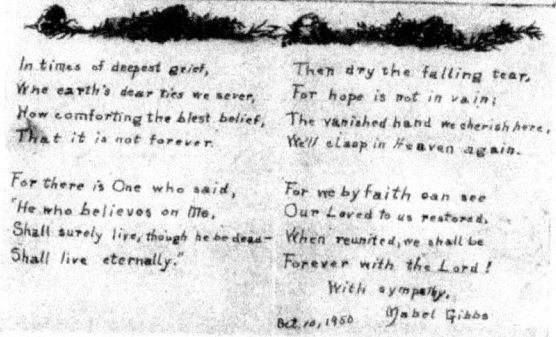

In times of deepest grief,
When earth's dear ties we sever,
How comforting the blest belief,
That it is not forever.

For there is One who said,
"He who believes in Me,
Shall surely live, though he be dead –
Shall live eternally."

Then dry the falling tear,
For hope is not in vain;
The vanished hand we cherish here,
We'll clasp in Heaven again.

For we by faith can see
Our loved to us restored,
When reunited, we shall be
Forever with the Lord!

With sympathy,

M.D.G.

After your fall,
and before start-
ing on your trip.
August 6, 1951
Morgantown, Wa.

I was sorry to hear of the accident,
That happened to you one day,
And hope that soon you'll be all right,
Always to stay that way.

But if a bit of sage advice,
Toward you I might direct:
Pray keep your equilibrium,
And always stand erect.

But should this feat be difficult.
Most arduous to do,
Have threatening upsets tip you off,
Thus tipped, no tips for you!

I wish you many great delights
On your journey to the West.
Of all the trips you ever had,
May this one be the best!
Mabel Gibbs

1951

I was sorry to hear of the accident,
That happened to you one day,
And hope that soon you'll be all right,
Always to stay that way.

But if a bit of sage advice,
Toward you I might direct:
Pray keep your equilibrium,
And always stand erect.

But should this feat be difficult
Most arduous to do
Have threatening upsets tip you off
Thus tipped, no tips for you!

I wish you many great delights
On your journey to the West
Of all the trips you ever had,
May this one be the best!

M.D.G.

To Mrs. W.E. King

On the death of her father when he was visiting

I pray that you may know,
I sympathize with you.
For I have no such comfort tho,
My heart was breaking, too.

We hear our Savior say,
"I'd never will forsake.
So, this you walk a lonely way,
You'll never be desolate.

Oh, I how who walked beside the sea,
And climbed Jardea's hill,
Who touched the hands outstretched to I thee
With balm for desperate ill's

Who quieted the tempest's roar
And multiplied the bread,
Who healed the leper's fatal sore
And brought to life the dead,

Oh, more today among the throngs,
With peace for all our life.
For still to thee, all powers belong
To give abundant life!

M.D.G

Moonshine

When we attempt to define anything, we usually want to know what Webster says about it. One of his definitions of moonshine is "a show without much reality." I once heard a Baptist minister say he would as soon lie down and let the moon shine in his mouth as to eat light bread. I think he must have had Webster's definition in mind.

But after we have gotten this definition, we come to the conclusion that it does [text cut off] usage of the word. In fact, we cannot define the word because the meaning is so different in different section of our country. When we hear the word sunshine we always think of the heat and light which it gives us, but what do we think of when we hear the word moonshine. As I have said everyone will not think of the same thing.

The Africans say "The moon is treacherous, trust not to her, for she will leave you stray," and instead of [text cut off]. When the moon is shining path, they gather close around their camp fire. But evidently all do not feel this way about it. Let us take a few instances that we may have a clearer idea of the different meanings of the word.

Up in the mountains of Kentucky, there lives an old man by the name of Joshua Hill. Go to him some day and ask him what the word moonshine means. Will he at once think of a calm night in autumn, when the moon is pursuing her oft trod path across the heavens, and not a sound is heard, save the rustling of the leaves, and loose murmuring voices tuned for the occasion! No, he will look you over carefully and if you can succeed in making him believe that you are not sent direct from Uncle Sam to pry in his affairs and ruin his business, he will perhaps leave you up the mountain by path that no one else could find, and to a cave that no one else knows of, and then he will explain to you what he understands by the word moonshine.

170

Take another instance. Down on the banks of one of our rivers, there lives a beautiful maiden and near her a handsome youth. Ask them what they think of when they hear the word moonshine. There will come before them, visions of many evening by the river's brink, when that satellite of the earth would slowly come higher and higher until it stood over a certain rustic willow chair and would gaze down at own reflected image in the water, and listen to the voices sweet and low. What were they two thinking of and of what were they talking? I will leave you to imagine that, but it was not a show without reality.

But coming closer home, what do the people of Maryville college think of when they hear the word moonshine? Do they think of similar circumstances to the above? I think not most of us have learned that when we cannot get what we prefer, must take the next best. The noble men and women unto whose hands, it has been our pleasant lot to be cast naturally, think we are here seeking all the light possible on all subjects, and as the light of the moon is only light borrowed from the sun, we are not supposed to allow it to be our guide while here. This is why we see so many converting day into night, as many would call it. But there is one characteristic of inhabitants of the land of real moonshine which we must not pass over low murmuring voices.

Perhaps I have not succeeded in defining moonshine. I believe each one will have to do this for himself. One thing I know, there is sometimes a reality, though it may not be visible, it is only felt by those who are deeply interested and pay the closest attention to the things which happen in this, my realm of moonshine.

About the Author

Yehuda "J.R." Rothstein is a real estate and construction counsel at an in-house tech company. Previously, he was a Fulbright visiting scholar at the University of Toronto Faculty of Law, where he focused on Comparative Real Estate transactions.

Mr. Rothstein is also a transactional attorney who practices on an extensive range of matters in both practice groups with both law firm and in-house counsel experience. His real estate law practice includes development, acquisitions and dispositions, and leasing transactions of real property. During his career, Mr. Rothstein has worked with numerous corporate and individual clients, including property managers, investors, developers, and cooperatives. He provides legal support and advice on all real estate matters. His legal advice goes beyond the law and responds creatively and strategically to meet business needs. Mr. Rothstein, who studies part-time real estate development at New York University, is a real estate investor himself and often assists his clients in syndicating real estate deals.

Mr. Rothstein received his Juris Doctor from Cornell Law School, where he was Editor of the Journal of Law and Public Policy and an Albert Heit Scholarship recipient. He simultaneously obtained an L.LM. Master of Laws in International and Comparative Law from Cornell Law. After

receiving his J.D. and L.LM., Mr. Rothstein began his legal career serving as a federal law clerk in the Eastern District of New York for the Honorable I. Leo Glasser. He later worked at a Midtown Manhattan law firm practicing real estate law.

Mr. Rothstein completed his undergraduate studies at the University of Michigan. After university, he was a Legacy

Heritage Fellow doing human rights at the United Nations. Later, Mr. Rothstein was an Ariana De Rothschild Fellow at the University of Cambridge Judge Business School in Cambridge, United Kingdom, focusing on Social Entrepreneurship and impact investing with faith-based communities.

Today, Mr. Rothstein is a member of DOROT, Sons of the American Revolution, and the NAACP. He also serves as a member of the Steering and Board of AJC ACCESS. Mr. Rothstein has lived, worked, studied, and traveled to over two dozen countries. He grew up in Monsey, New York.

www.ingramcontent.com/pod-product-compliance
Lightning Source LLC
Chambersburg PA
CBHW071116100726
47908CB00008B/2392